BEHIND MY WINGS

UNTOLD STORIES OF VIETNAM VETS

BJ ELLIOTT PRIOR
MAC STEWARDESS 1969-1971

WITH LINDA LOU COOMBS WIESE

Print History
Copyright © 2017 BJ Prior
ISBN: 978-1-940359-44-1
Library of Congress Control Number: 2017931945

Published by

www.BurkhartBooks.com

Bedford , Texas

WHAT VIETNAM VETS ARE SAYING ABOUT THE BOOK ...

Dear Flying Angel BJ, thank you for just a powerful story about myself. It really hit home. We all cried. It took a while to get through it. As you know telling people about Nam can never be the same as being there. As we landed in Nam we were on the ground, small arms fire, ran to the terminal floor, where we laid for two hours. Welcome to Nam. The scars of my memory never go away.

Michael Langan, US Army

Thank you, BJ, for taking the time and effort to write about my Vietnam experience. After retelling my Vietnam story, it brought healing and restoration not only for me, but also for my family. I am blessed to have such an awesome wife who had supported me through everything. To my children whom I love dearly, thanks for loving your dad as much as you do. It has meant the world to me. To my precious and strong grandchildren, loving you is a legacy that I cherish now and eternally.

David Stark, US Air Force

I saw your ad in the View, Sun City Apple Valley. I was in Vietnam 1966-67 with I Co. 3d Battalion, 26th Marines, (I Co. 3/26 Marines). When we left for Vietnam, there were 45 Marines in my platoon, 22 of us came back and all had been wounded at some point. I was wounded 4/27/67. I was retired with 100 percent disability from the wounds. There isn't a day that doesn't go by that I'm back in Vietnam. Overall I feel blessed.

Michael Mulraney, USMC

"Brothers, I do not consider myself yet to have taken hold of it. But one thing I do; Forgetting what is behind and straining toward what is ahead"
Philippines 3:13

DEDICATION

IN LOVING MEMORY OF

Carlton and "Mom" Connie Angell
Dad, Thomas O. Elliott and Grandparents
Tom Schuchat
Sheri Carlson
Marty and Helen Jay

Carlton and my mother married late in life; Mom was 90 when she passed, and Carlton was 95. Carlton always encouraged me to write my book.

My dad, Thomas Elliott, was a kind and gentle man. My Grandmother, Jane was a pioneer woman who looked after us along with my Spanish grandparents.

Tom Schuchat was one of our fun-loving pilots who served in Vietnam and was later hired by Continental Airlines. He also flew the military flights back to Vietnam as the 2nd Officer on many of my flights. He later became a friend when he married a co-worker friend of mine. I share his story.

Sheri Carlson was a dear friend and co-worker (flight attendant) who continually urged me to finish my book. She fought the good fight, but her battle with cancer took her before I completed it. You would be proud Sheri! I did change the title of the book as you suggested. Thank you, miss you.

Marty and Helen Jay were an awesome couple that I met in my twenties during my Hollywood era. Marty was a librarian and Helen was his vivacious, fun-loving wife. While I was Brenda Star at the Hollywood Citizen Newspaper, Helen was one of my best customers. Thank you for inviting me over to your lovely Hollywood Hills home. You'll never know how much I appreciated your love and friendship.

ACKNOWLEDGMENTS

"In Everything Give Thanks"
1 Thessalonians 5:18

I wish to thank my family and friends whose encouragement helped me to write this book. I wish to thank foremost my loving husband of 41 years for your patience when I was too consumed with writing to cook dinner. Thank you for helping me to go deeper with my feelings and dealing with my past, I love you.

To my dear friend, who is like a sister, Linda Lou Coombs Wiese. Thank you for being my co-writer and spending hours helping me write and rewrite, verifying names, places, and dates. Thank you for allowing me to cry while reading each of the men's stories.

To Professor George Yancey and his wife Drommie, an English teacher, thank you for the length of time you gave to me with your coaching and training. Your classes on "Do the Write Thing" encouraged and helped me with the passion that was laid buried in my heart. I would also like to acknowledge two very special ladies, Audrey Wyatt and Bettie Williams, who helped me with copyrights, editing, and gave me valuable input.

A special acknowledgment to my son-in-law, Captain John Brancato, US Army, for your service and for your help editing the final manuscript.

I wish to acknowledge all the Military Airlift Command (MAC) flight attendants who shared some of their Vietnam stories, and I wish to thank a very special group of retired flight attendants, the Dallas Golden Penguins for your continual support and love. You are awesome ladies!

To my Covenant Church family whom I love dearly. To our Retired Pastor Mike Hayes and my Colleyville Pastor Ricky Texada, thank you both for your words of encouragement to write this book and to offer seminars and classes to prepare me to write. To my special group of Senior Ladies who allowed me, their leader, to be off during the summer months to focus and write my book, I love each of you very much.

And MOST of all to the Vietnam Vets who served our country despite the turmoil and riots in America. Thank you for your service and for all you sacrificed. America did not realize your conflicts and inner battles, both abroad and here at home. You are the brave men and women, my heroes. It was an honor to serve you on the MAC flights. You helped me to be brave while taking you over, and you allowed me to see your tired, vulnerable selves on the flights back home. I am forever grateful to each of you. Welcome Home!

CONTENTS

Continental Airlines did not have Row 13, so I opted not to have a Chapter 13

I lift up my eyes to the hills
Where does my help come from?
My help comes from the Lord,
The Maker of heaven and earth.

Psalms 121:1 NIV

INTRODUCTION

During the era when flight attendants were called stewardesses, I saw the best and the worst of times in our country. In the sixties, we entered a war that brought permanent changes in our culture and society. From 1969-1971, I was an impressionable young stewardess transporting troops to the battlefields of Vietnam. My heart was stirred deeply as young soldiers fresh out of boot camp full of life, bravely faced the ravages of war.

As a new stewardess, I was looking for glamor, adventure, and travel. My professional and proper dress was in stark contrast to the fatigues the soldiers wore. We each proudly wore them during this combustible time in history. My story together with Vietnam Vets weaves a tapestry of pain, sorrow, courage and strength. As our lives intersected, each soldier we left in Vietnam made an indelible imprint on my life and the lives of other stewardesses. We made the most of our flights and partied hard to forget. Love affairs on layovers tempered the heaviness and sadness I felt during those two years. Beneath the uniform with gloves, hat, and my wings, was a heart of gratitude for the opportunity to serve brave soldiers who sacrificed so much.

There is an appointed time for everything
And there is a season for every activity under Heaven:
A time to be born and a time to die,
A time to plant and a time to uproot,
A time to kill and a time to heal,
A time to tear down and a time to build,
A time to weep and a time to laugh,
A time to mourn and a time to dance
A time to scatter stones and a time to gather them,
A time to embrace and a time to refrain
A time to search and a time to give up,

A time to keep and a time to throw away,
A time to tear and a time to mend,
A time to be silent and a time to speak,
A time to love and a time to hate,
A time for war and a time for peace.

Ecclesiastes 3:1-8 NIV

This scripture motivated me to write my memoirs of Vietnam and to tell the stories of our military and their private battles, as well as mine. History needs to be told, including the battles and the emotions soldiers experienced, the incredible odds of their survival. Though they still may have PTSD these soldiers are NOT weak; they are indeed mighty. I would count them as strong individuals and am proud to be their friend then and now.

Per Webster's New World College Dictionary: PTSD (Post-traumatic stress disorders) is a condition characterized by recurring and often disabling symptoms of anxiety and depression that later affects some persons who have experienced a traumatic event or situation, especially in combat. As an eyewitness to history, I bring to light the stories of forgotten vets. The stain and the scars of this troublesome war will be forever embedded in American history. Etched in my heart are the Vietnam Veterans who will always remain heroes. I wrote *Behind My Wings* to enlighten the past, present, and future generations that during the battles of not only war but in life, there remains hope for our country, love for each other and faith in our God. I ask readers to honor these heroes with me as we touch their scars and embrace their pain.

VIETNAM WAR SYNOPSIS

The war in Vietnam was between the communist North Vietnam and the struggle for independence and freedom for South Vietnam. The United States came to the aide of the South Vietnamese as early as 1955 when President Dwight Eisenhower sent advisors. In 1961, President John F. Kennedy increased involvement of the CIA (Central Intelligent Agency) and US Ambassadors. Vice President Lyndon B Johnson was sworn in as President in 1963, the same day of the assassination of Kennedy. Time for war came when President Lyndon B. Johnson sent US troops in 1964. He contracted commercial airliners to transport combat troops into Vietnam. Thus boots on the ground began military involvement. We were full-fledged into the war with our military bases strategically located in South Vietnam.

The Vietnam War was during a time of racial conflicts, political disillusionment, the onset of illicit drugs and the sexual revolution. Perhaps you were there, perhaps not; perhaps you were not yet born. Regardless, most readers are unaware of the tragedies and triumphs of this strange and far away war. The United States spent two long decades in racial unrest, along with the heart-wrenching Vietnam War. A counter-culture called the "hippies" advocated non-violence. Drugs accentuated the hippie movement along with the advent of "free love" and the introduction of birth control pills. The hippies vehemently opposed the Vietnam War by demonstrating in antiwar protests and marches. The war became unpopular, and as it continued into the late sixties, Americans witnessed the rise of protesters, rioters, and demonstrators in cities and universities. During the same time frame, the country faced racial challenges. A root of hatred led to the assassinations of key leaders like Martin Luther King and Robert Kennedy, the brother of

President John F. Kennedy who had been assassinated a few years earlier.

This war caused the already over-taxed emotional state of the country to rise to a fever pitch. As riots and demonstrations continued to grow, the National Guard was called to help control the protesters. The Vietnam War was a defining moment when America shunned their Vets. I lived during this tumultuous setting with thousands of young men my age or younger being drafted or enlisted, my brother being one who enlisted. Finally, in 1973 President Richard Nixon, with the help of Henry Kissinger, signed a Peace Treaty in exchange for the cease- fire and the return of all POW's and MIA's (Prisoners of War and Missing in Action). A time for peace, as difficult as it had been, finally came in 1975. The stain and the scars of this unpopular war will be forever embedded in our history.

Chapter One

FACING HEADWINDS

Descending into the black, thick jungle below, the silence in the aircraft felt heavy and foreboding. Night flying was as dark as the evil below, revealing the horrors of war. Only the low roar of the engines could break the deafening silence of the night as we looked out the windows watching the vivid scenes of bombs lighting up the ground. DaNang was the most intimidating, fearful and uncertain territories to land in Vietnam. Our flights were in the early mornings while it was still dark and because we could visually see the bombings below, it became one of the places that I hated to land.

As we descended, the men began their preparation for landing. They kept their emotions within, but we witnessed the changes in their faces as they became combat ready. Our descent was rapid, and the explosions on the ground appeared close. There was an eerie silence hovering over the cabin as the wheels lowered; we knew this was our time to take our jump seats. With 165 soldiers on board, we felt protected landing in this warzone. With an abrupt touchdown, stairs were brought to the airplane for both the rear and front doors. As we opened our exits, the men stood up, ready to deplane at a fast pace. Putting our hats and gloves on, we were the first to go down the stairs even though the company wanted us to remain on board. We said our goodbyes at the bottom of the stairs. The men moved fast down the stairs, their boots hitting the tarmac with loud thuds and they were gone from our sights. We felt the exploding bombs vibrate the ground under our feet and prepared to run to the bunkers with the soldiers who met the aircraft.

Fast forward to 1994, *Forrest Gump* was not just a great movie, but a poignant moment for me. Exiting the theater with my husband, I began to sob uncontrollably. My memories of flying the troops into Vietnam surfaced, and flashbacks flooded me as I saw the reunion of Forrest Gump and Lieutenant Dan, who had lost both of his legs from the war. All my memories and emotions were as though they had been locked up in a time capsule, ready to explode. My husband held me in his arms, not realizing that this movie unveiled so many emotions. He kept asking me, "What's wrong?" I couldn't stop crying and realized all the feelings that I had suppressed for years now surfaced. I am sure the people leaving the movie theater thought we were fighting.

It was then, at this pivotal point that I realized how the Vietnam war had affected me. I came to understand and experience my own Post-Traumatic Stress Disorder (PTSD). I served not as a soldier but as a stewardess transporting the soldiers to Vietnam. This is my story and those of men of "valor." The years from 1994 until I retired in 2008 were completely occupied with the care of my elderly parents. When they both passed away, the passion for writing culminated in 2012 when I discovered many from my high school served in Vietnam. It was then I delved deeply into my memory bank to uncover the emotions and the stories of my classmates. I write now to hopefully bring some closure and healing, not only to the many brave soldiers but also to myself. Today is my time and my season to write. May God touch each and every one who reads this book.

Chapter Two

RUNWAYS OF LIFE

Before I formed you in the womb I knew you,
before you were born I set you apart.
Jeremiah 1:5 NIV

My childhood was quite different from most; I grew up in the 40s and 50s with deaf parents. My world created many challenges. The deaf world is a close group. My parents had many friends and family members who were deaf. They belonged to the Los Angeles Club for the Deaf, and my mother was involved with numerous activities and parties. As a CODA (child of deaf parents) you become the interpreter, their ears, an advocate and problem solver. The deaf world was truly silent for me growing up as we had no TV, radio or telephone and little money. Living in the deaf culture, I found it hard to relate to the hearing world. As difficult as it was, I would not have traded my childhood because growing up with the deaf community enhanced my sensitivity to life. Sign language is a beautiful communication, not only using your hands and fingers but facial expressions as well. I am so thankful to have grown up surrounded by so many wonderful and dear family friends of my parents. I am at times still able and drawn to sign worship songs at my church.

The deaf community was tight-knit. Unfortunately, my parents' marriage was not. A defining moment in time was the night my mother left my father. Their marriage had always been estranged. I will always remember that distressful night. We were living in Hollywood with my grandmother, my father's mother and during an argument between my parents, my mom started to leave. When I ask,

"Where are you going?" she signed and said, "I am leaving your father because I feel desperate and hopeless." Right at that moment, I signed to her, "I am coming with you." It was scary for me as a six- year-old child making this life-changing decision. That night, my mother and I walked to the bus stop on Hollywood Boulevard. My mother's crying kept my tears silent as we waited for the bus. My dad's heart was broken, and my older sister and younger brother did not even know that my mother and I had left.

Those first few weeks after leaving my dad and siblings I felt all alone and isolated. Friends of the family took us in until my mom was able to rent a motel room and pay rent on a weekly basis. Supporting us on the meager wages of a seamstress was very difficult for my mom. She struggled to make the $23.00 weekly rent. When times became too difficult, she took me to Arizona to live with my grandparents, who spoke only Spanish. Although they could not communicate, they cared for me for nearly a year while my mother worked in Los Angeles. I played outside, helped my grandparents and walked to the Catholic Church every week with fresh flowers from my grandmother's garden. There was a surreal peaceful feeling I encountered each time at the altar. I can't explain, but it was as though I belonged there in God's presence. I loved replacing the old flowers with grandma's fresh flowers. It left a fresh smell, and I liked leaving the altar clean. I was just a child, yet I enjoyed this chore.

When my mother came back for me, she was shocked to see that I had lost weight, but in all actuality, I had grown, and my dresses were now shorter on me. My mom and I took the train back to Los Angeles. My years at school were quite difficult. I started school late—no one knew if I had gone to first grade? Somehow, I survived, even when held back in the fourth grade at a Catholic school.

My mother eventually divorced my dad when I was seven years old. She dated several men and four years later remarried a younger man. He and my mother came home and announced they had driven to Mexico and got married. He told me his last name and how to spell it. It was a very short courtship. My step dad could speak, but he spoke loud because of his deafness. He had polio at the age of nine and nearly died at the time, but he remembers God speaking to him during the night, saying it's not your time yet. When he woke up, he had lost his hearing from the effects of polio. Fortunately, he could use his voice but spoke loud. He and mom seemed to be happy. We moved from our small place into a unit that had a separate sleeping room. He began to help me with my homework, and we all were settling into this new family living. My mom and step-dad both worked and after school, I would come home and begin preparing rice to add to the main dish that my mom would fix for dinner.

Along with these family changes, I was soon to experience a foretaste of future changes in my life. When I was 13, I was still quite skinny and gawky. My closest friend had moved to Sacramento, and her parents invited me to come for a visit. When I asked my parents, to my surprise, they said yes. Nothing in those days was easy for deaf people; communicating with the hearing world was almost impossible. This was before the service of the TTY, where they could type messages on the phone. They had to write out everything to a hearing person. They went to the airport to purchase the ticket for me, and I was thrilled. My mother made the clothes that I wore on the flight and I wore my buckle shoes with white short socks. She packed my suitcase and added a lot of snack foods in case I got hungry while at their home. I was excited to visit my friend but not sure how I would react to flying. It was a night flight, and I was given a window seat.

The takeoff was thrilling. I was mesmerized by the whole event and could not take my eyes off all the city lights that twinkled below. The silhouette of the moon kept breaking in and out of the clouds, and it was breath taking. As I continued to look out the window, I felt exhilarated like my first time at Disneyland. A new passion stirred in my heart, little did I know the dramatic effect this flight would have on my life. When I timidly got up to use the restroom, the stewardess was walking down the aisle, and I remember as if it were yesterday, saying excitedly to her, "When I grow up, I am going to be an Air Hostess just like you!" It was such an unexpected and profound statement that flew out of my mouth. I startled myself when I said it. She said nothing, not even a smile, only a blank look staring back at me. My heart sank, thoughts rushed into my head, maybe I was not pretty enough, too skinny or gawky, or maybe she saw my bowed legs? But God had planted His seed and purpose for my life on that flight.

Returning home was difficult, my stepfather's discipline became harsh, and with his raised voice he began to yell at my mother and me. To escape the unhappiness, after doing my chores, I quickly would play outdoors with the neighborhood kids. My parents would go out often on Saturday nights to the bars or deaf clubs. I learned to occupy my time home alone. They returned after having several drinks and slept in the following mornings. I spent a lot of time alone, and maybe that is why I immersed myself in school activities. I liked being around all the kids. The elementary school that I was attending was having elections for the student body officers. I decided to run for President. There were several who also ran for the same office, but to my surprise, I was elected President. I enjoyed being on the school board representing the students and learned a lot about Parliamentary procedures.

This involvement at the school didn't last long as we began moving from one city to another city, largely due to my stepfather's jobs. We had moved two more times, which caused me to go to three different high schools within a two-year period. At each high school, I would just begin to make friends when we would have to move again. These were very difficult years, and some strange things were developing at home with my stepfather's affections towards me.

We had moved to Hawthorne, California, which was near the beaches in Los Angeles. They enrolled me at Hawthorne High School, where the Beach Boys had been attending. The Beach Boys were already popular and performed at various places and cities. It was a great high school with a winning football team, an excellent music/arts department and outstanding scholastic achievements. In this uplifting and encouraging atmosphere, I slowly began to make friends. I became involved in school activities, took all my classes seriously and attended the football games. The encouragement from the student body along with the help from teachers built my confidence. I blossomed in my studies and even made the honor roll.

With new friends and spending much time at the beaches, I wanted to learn to surf but was forbidden by my step-dad. He had become a weekend alcoholic, and it was during this time that he began making unhealthy advances. When I would tell my mom, they would fight, but he never changed. It was horrible, and I remained silent and shameful, unable to share with anyone. I once again immersed myself in school activities. My veneer of a good student at school hid my emotional turmoil at home. My home life kept deteriorating, frantic and needing a safe place to live, at 16, I moved to my grandmother's house in Hollywood. My sister and brother had been living with her since the divorce. I was determined not to change high schools again and wanted to finish my senior year at Hawthorne High. The boy I was dating joined the Air Force and would be gone for nearly a year. He allowed me to drive his '57 Chevy back and forth to school. It was a stick shift, turquoise and would turn heads today.

After graduating from Hawthorne High School, I applied at the lustrous Hollywood Citizen Newspaper. I was hired for the classified department and took the name Brenda Star. Surrounded by nurturing women, they taught me about writing ads and conversing with people. They were an inspiration to me for six years. For a high school graduate, it paid well.

I distinctly and vividly remember the day when a young clerk came down the spiral staircase at the newspaper and shouted to all of us that the President of the United States had been shot in Dallas, Texas. It was November 22, 1963. Within hours, we learned that President John F. Kennedy died from an assassination wound to his head. The whole world was stunned and in disbelief. America was changed that year because of this tragic event. This was the beginning of chaos in the 60s.

Amongst this tumultuous time, I had some rough times in my personal life as well. I ended up marrying my boyfriend when he returned from the service. Deep down, I knew I married out of guilt over premarital sex, instead of love. Somewhere inside me, I was searching to fill a void in my life. I brought all my childhood/teenage hang-ups into the marriage. Our marriage ended after two years, but it took another year for the divorce to be final in the state of California.

My salary at the Hollywood Citizen Newspaper afforded me a lush Hollywood apartment, which led me to move right into the Hollywood singles lifestyle. I frequently ate at the Hollywood Brown Derby and dressed like a model. I even had grandiose ideas of becoming an actress or model. I interviewed with agents and prepared a portfolio with questionable photos, all taken in hopes of being discovered. Years later, I was horrified to find out that certain photos had been sold on the black market, and to my regret, resurfaced several years later in Vietnam..

A silver lining to my dating life in Hollywood led me to a man who worked for Continental Airlines. I shared with him my desire to be a stewardess. He said he could not get me the job but would bring me an application. God was directing my path even though I was not walking with Him. You could not be married as a stewardess, and when I had applied with Continental Airlines, I had just started my divorce proceedings. They told me to reapply in a year when my divorce was final. I continued to work at the Hollywood newspaper and gave my boss a year's notice. We all laughed, but in my heart, I knew I would be hired as a stewardess.

My passion was so strong that I took classes at local colleges to learn French and Spanish. But my dating life kept me too busy to focus seriously. Thus both of these languages remain dormant. I also had an entrepreneurial spirit that led me to run ads for roommates, sharing an oceanfront house that I found for rent in Manhattan Beach. I was able to run free ads in our newspaper and ended up with over twenty females coming and going at different times to enjoy a day or weekend at the beach. They were career gals who also lived in Hollywood and loved the idea of going to the beach on their days off. Rent was always shared depending on how many we had each month, but after one year, I relinquished it to the remaining gals. The experience of being an entrepreneur gave me more confidence for my new career.

PRE-FLIGHT

The second interview with Continental Airlines went smoothly for me, but after leaving the interview, I said a little prayer, "God, please help me to get this job; I promise to always be a good stewardess." Qualifications to become a stewardess consisted mainly of appearance, height, weight and interpersonal abilities. The skills built in me at a young age interpreting for my deaf parents, along with my career with the Hollywood Citizen Newspaper, gave me confidence as well as abilities to interact with different people. I am not sure what part of the interview got me the job, but I can honestly say, God, did answer my prayer. I was hired in March 1968 but opted to start my Air Hostess training class in May. Saying my goodbyes to the awesome women who worked with me in the Classified Department was bittersweet. They knew my desire to become an air hostess and wished me well. In those days, the airline called us air hostesses later we were called stewardesses and finally, flight attendants.

Happy and nervous, I entered the longest four weeks of my life. Our class began with 42 ladies who were as anxious as I was on that very first day. Early in our processing, we were asked to select a president; many could have fulfilled that position, but I was nominated. At 24, I was representing 41 extraordinary ladies from various backgrounds and lifestyles. Some with camouflaged secrets, such as mine, married and divorced. One gal discovered she was pregnant during training and had to leave. Remember, you could not be married or have children.

Continental Airlines' training program both for Pilots and Air Hostess was one of the best. The professional and polished air hostess trainers expected the same in us. There was no margin for error; we soon learned that mistakes or flaws were not tolerated. Between spontaneous testing and grooming mishaps, some girls were released. Every one of us had our hair cut the same way, short and above the collar. Those who refused were let go. We soon found out that any complaining regarding our hotel or lack of transportation to shop for uniform items resulted in being terminated.

As their President, I wanted to look and dress my best, so when I ran out of clothes, my girlfriend Bonnie loaned me some great outfits to finish the remaining weeks. Our training days were filled with FAA (Federal Aviation Administration) rules and regulations along with the policies and procedures of Continental Airlines. Part of our training was how to accentuate our appearances, to be poised and proper at all times. A day's makeup session consisted of a foundation, Day Dew, used by movie stars. It was suggested to wear false eyelashes, bras that gave a lift, and girdles to shape us. Our evenings were crammed with studies, meals, and little sleep. Back in those days, we shared our rooms with another classmate, and that continued until the male hosts were hired and required their own single rooms. Thus the company policy changed in the early 70s.

During those four weeks of training, we learned to ditch a raft in the ocean, open emergency exits, deploy slides and memorize emergency equipment on every aircraft that Continental had in their fleet. We had to learn city codes and military time and FAA regulations, which filled my every waking hour. We were now prepared to handle emergency conditions from evacuating the aircraft to delivering babies—both incidences happened during my career. Our training was worth its weight in gold, which proved to be necessary when a crisis arose. Our manuals became our sidekick, and we were required to carry them while working. Our training days flew by so quickly that it was difficult to get to know everyone. Even after graduation, I still met some in my class who I did not know well. The ongoing pressure of the daily training consumed us. However, just like high school or college, we bonded and celebrated at our graduation.

For a girl who grew up in Hollywood, hats, pearls and gloves fit the way I wanted to look, stylish and pretty. Surviving in Hollywood and now as an air hostess required more than a look, as I had to learn to be resourceful, alert, and knowledgeable. I was ready for the long-awaited career. For the 31 of us who finally made it to graduation day, we had a sense of accomplishment and camaraderie which lasted our entire career—some a lifetime.

Chapter Three

ALTITUDE CHECK

Dormitory living in an affluent and sophisticated apartment began my flying career. Roommates came and went at all different hours, sharing lives and expenses. The entry hall of our apartment was wallpapered with business cards given to us from admiring passengers. We were flattered, yet never called them. Traveling by air in the 60s and 70s was a grandiose event with men in ties and ladies in dresses. It was not just a flight but also an experience, choices of hot meals delivered with a professional touch, smile, and conversation.

Unfortunately, the nine months of domestic flying found me in the lavatory throwing up. I felt like I was on a roller coaster, especially with the turbulence flying into Denver, Colorado.

Air hostess school never mentioned the possibility of air sickness. I had serious thoughts of quitting during these first few months, but with the encouragement of my mother, I continued to fly. Needing a desperate change from the short hop flights, I signed up for the military flights. The government chartered Continental as well as other airlines to fly our military troops to Vietnam. The aircraft on these flights were Boeing 707's with four jet engines, cabin capacity of 165 passenger seating, three pilots in the cockpit, and four stewardesses in the cabin.

These flights were called Military Airlift Command or better known as the MAC flights. The flights for our airline originated from the West Coast military bases to Hawaii, Guam, Philippines, Okinawa, Japan, Taiwan, Korea, South Vietnam and Bangkok. In some cases, we landed in various other bases when fuel or maintenance was required. In Vietnam, Continental flew mainly into Saigon, DaNang, and Cam Ranh Bay. In rare situations, we would land at the military base in Bien Hoa.

Shortly after signing up, I was awarded the MAC flights. Preparation began immediately, starting with a series of shots for every known disease, followed by briefing instructions, such as the use of bunkers during bombings while at the military bases. We were given orders not to deplane whenever in Vietnam unless directed by the ground military personnel. We carried an identification card given to us by the government of the United States which listed our name and rank as 2nd Lieutenant in the United States Air Force. We were told if the enemy captured us, with officer status, we would be treated fairly. We doubted the validity of that statement.

Despite the danger, I was ready and prepared for the long flights, anxious now to serve our military troops but not prepared for the emotional toll of what I was about to experience. I eagerly waited for the phone call from scheduling to assign me my first trip. When the call came, I had two days to pack; we were told that we should pack for at least a week as most of the trips were from six to eight days long. We were given a large suitcase without wheels, luggage with wheels had not been invented yet, plus a garment bag for our uniforms. Driving to the LAX airport, my nerves and excitement consumed me. Checking in with scheduling, we had to sign in and show all our IDs, including our passport. We then were transported directly to the aircraft parked away from the terminals. Our luggage was placed in the belly before boarding the aircraft. I was met by the seasoned pilots and stewardesses who guided me through all the necessary pre-departure procedures. The Captain gave us a briefing, and we ferried the empty aircraft out of Los Angeles to Travis Air Force base.

The date was March 8, 1969. As the soldiers boarded the aircraft, I could not help but notice how young they looked. Right out of boot camp, their disciplinary actions and strength were very impressive. There were no class dividers on these aircraft; every soldier was treated like first class. As a young stewardess, I was honored to serve them. It was a virgin flight for me as well as for them, and even though I was excited to be on these MAC flights, I also was looking forward to my first layover in Hawaii. With engines roaring and wheels up, there I sat in my jump seat facing 165 soldiers. I will always remember that first flight; I was in awe. Fortunately, my duties overtook my nervousness. The flight time to Hawaii was five and a half hours and did not seem long. I remember it was pleasant, fun and light-hearted. Best of all, I did not get sick on descent. After landing, the soldiers deplaned but only long enough for the aircraft to be cleaned and replenished with new meals. Their next leg would be just over 11 hours to the Philippines. Their flight to Vietnam, depending upon which base they flew to, would be another three hours. As I deplaned in Hawaii, along with the other crew members, the beautiful plush, balmy weather felt wonderful to my skin and hair. I was looking forward to the three-day layover, barefoot in my bathing suit on the beaches of Waikiki. Prior to our landing, the First Officer asked me to go to a movie that first night. I politely declined thinking to myself, "My first night in Hawaii, I wanted to be on the beach not in a movie theater." Besides, he was married, however, the following night found us at a quiet dinner overlooking the beaches of Waikiki. So, began wartime romances that had no boundaries.

The following days I spent sunbathing on the beach and thought to myself, this was paradise and I could see myself enjoying these MAC flights. The company paid for our hotel, and we received per diem that paid for our meals. We stayed at the Reef Hotel which was right on the beach. They had a bar underground that had a window to the hotel's pool. The first time I swam in that pool, I was unaware of the audience who could see everything. This bar became one of our hangouts. In the years to follow, Hawaii held mostly secret romances.

Our next scheduled assignment came after three days; my body was sunburned, but I prepared myself for an early morning flight to the Philippines. This trip was going to be my first long eleven-hour flight. After checking everything in our pre-departure procedures, we were ready to board the troops. After the previous five-and-a-half-hour flight to Hawaii, the troops filing on board appeared subdued and tired. They were courteous and at times talkative. We served them two meals, along with multiple beverage services. This was a time before we had meal or beverage carts. Since everything was hand-carried, I quickly learned how to carry several food and beverage trays at one time.

I was exhausted after that flight and looked forward to the layover in the Philippines. Landing in this far away country at Clark Air Base, to my delight the weather was warm and humid. Driving off the base to our hotel, I noticed the houses on base were on stilts with a wraparound enclosed screened-porch. Intrigued, I soon learned of their monsoons rains that brought about flash flooding, requiring the houses to be on stilts to keep them safe from the rising water. The company had us staying at the Oasis Hotel which was just outside the gates of the base. It was a nice hotel with all the amenities. We were given privileges to go back on base to the Officers' Club, where drinks were only seventy-five cents. Most of my time during this layover was spent at the pool. So far I had been able to enjoy adventures and relaxation, but soon, I would come face to face with the realities of war.

Chapter Four

DESCENT, PRESSURE WITHIN

The war was far from my mind as I sunbathed on the beaches of Hawaii and at the poolside in the Philippines. Little did I know this next flight was going to be such a rude awakening for me. After a few days in the Philippines, we were alerted about our next flight assignment which was going to be to Saigon. This is what I signed up for, and now I would be flying my first trip to Vietnam. The set time allowed us to prepare properly, meaning stop drinking and get some sleep. We had to pack all our belongings— everything always traveled with us. Again, I had yet to come to grips with the incredible reality of war.

As the men re-boarded the aircraft in the Philippines, their demeanor had changed from that first flight out of California. To my surprise, the flight time was nearly three hours which gave us time to serve them one last hot meal. It was my first flight into Vietnam, and I sensed some nervousness among the soldiers. These young men just traveled nearly twenty-two hours and their D-Day was coming to fruition. They no doubt had many thoughts, even prayers, as the aircraft descended through the clouds. As we prepared for landing, walking through the cabin, I noticed some were making the sign of the cross while most were looking out the windows, surmising the terrain as best as they could from the air. They realized they soon would be facing all kinds of battles in this foreign land

As I looked out the window, we were flying over rice paddies. I saw the surrounding thick jungle and my detached feelings now began to surface. After we landed, the men methodically grabbed their head gear and other belongings. As they began to deplane, I was in a state of numbness. They were off to war, and I didn't say good-bye.

What words could I have said to them as I stared at the empty cabin? I was feeling such an emptiness. The lump in my throat began to tighten and not wanting anyone to see me cry; I fled into the cockpit. Alone, with the door closed, I burst into tears. The reality of war hit me. When I stopped crying, I told myself I would never let my emotions show when the soldiers deplaned in Vietnam. As I came out of the cockpit, the other stewardesses were tidying the aircraft. They informed me that we clean the aircraft in Vietnam because the Vietnamese were not allowed on board. The airline could not trust anyone, and we were satisfied with that decision.

Our ground time was very short, long enough to deplane and tidy the cabin. The new meals were retrieved from the cargo bins and brought up to both galleys. The men, anxious to fly out, were already boarding. They quickly took their seats, starting from the rear of the aircraft, filling each row. There was a mixture of soldier's fatigues; some looked like they just came from the jungle, stained with an orange residue on their fatigues while others were clean. Their somber faces matched their weary bodies. I couldn't help but recall the statement from the Statue of Liberty that says; "Give me your tired, your poor, your huddled masses yearning to breathe free." At that very moment, as I welcomed them on board, I was thankful to be a part of this military operation realizing war is hell.

As we prepared to take off, there seemed to be an apprehension felt by all of us. Beginning our taxi down the runway with full throttle and flaps up, we gained speed for take-off. The moment the wheels retracted into the fuselage, applause roared through the cabin. Breathing a sigh of relief, we felt incredibly safe and secure. Thus, began my Military Airlift Command (MAC) journey flights that brought me sadness along with a real sense of duty.

FLIGHTS AND LAYOVERS

Continental Airlines began the Military Airlift Command (MAC) operations in 1964 with two new Boeing 707-320's aircraft with flights to Hawaii, Guam, Philippines, Japan, Taiwan, Korea, Okinawa, South Vietnam, and Thailand. This MAC contract was a busy service transporting the American troops in and out of Vietnam. I flew into most the designated countries, some more frequently than others, depending on the greatest need for soldiers. 70 to 80 US bases had been built inside South Vietnam. Vietnam sanctuaries or safe places were established on Laos and Cambodia borders.

As I mentioned, my very first flight was into Saigon where the airport seemed small with only one tower. Towards the end of my MAC flights, that small tower in Saigon had been blown up. If you were to look at a photo of the airport today, it is very modern, quite large and it is called Tan Son Nhat International Airport.

Cam Ranh Bay was nice. I had no idea that because of the heat during the day, the runways needed nightly repairs. But to me, it seemed the safest, even though they found bullet holes in our fuselage. I had always wondered in the two years of flying in and out of Vietnam, could we have been shot down or blown up? In interviewing several Vietnam Vets, they told me about the double protection around the perimeter of all our airfields by the South Korean Army. Our government paid a higher wage to their soldiers than their government to protect the bases from an attack of the Viet Cong.

Guam was another landing place; however, we did not have very many trips there. Back in the 60s, it was still sparsely populated. The one and only hotel was near a peninsula where we could walk way out in the ocean waters. I remember they had cucumber urchins and you did not want to step on them. The beach water was warm because it was so shallow until the tide would come in.

Several times we flew trips into Bangkok, Thailand. Our ground time was short but we had allowed enough time to eat or shop at their small airport. The hot, humid weather caused one to sweat immediately. The whole crew would rush to the restaurant and order the spicy Mongolian BBQ beef. Our sweating was enhanced by eating this meal—it was superb!

Returning to our aircraft and boarding our troops, we headed to Vietnam. Vietnam's weather was like nearby regions and countries. There were two major monsoon seasons in South Vietnam. It rains heavily from May to September and from November to March. In the dry season, many swampy areas in the monsoon turn to dust. Wet and dry seasons varied considerably in both time and intensity from area to area.

Bien Hoa was never an easy place to land. Though all warzones were hazardous, Bien Hoa was terribly dangerous. Our pilots were the best! Casting fear aside, they used much wisdom with each flight into Bien Hoa. We trusted them, and they did their jobs well. One Captain made the decision to take off despite mortar and rocket attacks. He commented, "These guys fought for us, I am getting them the hell out of this place." It was full throttle ahead. Once airborne, the awesome applause from the men in the cabin was deafening. Continental, as well as all other contracted airlines, never lost an aircraft.

Weather conditions and high activity in Nam, caused our flight schedules to change constantly. Unscheduled landings found us in difficult situations, and our Captains sometimes would use their own credit cards to pay for the aircraft's fuel or departure fees. One specific stop would not take the credit card, so the whole crew had to use all the cash they had to pay the bill. Robert F. Six, the owner of Continental Airlines was a maverick, and his pilots had to step up in many situations to be able to leave a country. Hawaii to the Philippines or Okinawa became our fun-filled flights. Because of the length of these flights, we could enjoy ourselves, laughing while playing jokes and games. Our flights had just one branch on board, Marines or Army though occasionally we would have a lone warrior from the Air Force or Navy. However, out of Vietnam, we would have high-ranking officials, generals or colonels. We loved all the branches and had one innocent prank we liked to play on them. After they ate and before we picked up their trays, we would approach one soldier and say, "We need your help in the aft galley, could you help us?" Immediately they would come back to the galley. We then would put one of our aprons and wigs on them. We still could not let our hairline touch our collar, so many of us wore wigs, hair pieces to keep in compliance with the company's regulations. We then gave them a pot of coffee and sent them out in the aisle. Soon the roar of hilarious laughter began to fill the cabin. We so enjoyed letting them have this moment of fun, hopefully, and for a moment it took their minds off their destination. These aircraft were not modern; movie projectors had not been designed into them. We were their entertainment, and we took this job seriously.

When nighttime came, most would sleep, but as we strolled the aisle, finding one or two still awake and not able to sleep, we would invite them back to the galley area to play cards. Because space was tight on these aircraft, we had some room just in front of the aft jump seat. We would lay a blanket on the floor where we would sit and play poker or blackjack until we got tired. These flights were long, sometimes grueling, but our memories of time with the men will always remain in our hearts. There was never any disruption from these soldiers; not once did these men cause any problems. America would have been proud of these men. War is never easy, but these men served—many would not return home. As crew members, we knew the reality; that's why we bonded so easily with these soldiers. They were our guys, our heroes who were going to war.

Okinawa, the fifth largest island of Japan, was the processing station. We transported the troops out of Vietnam to Okinawa where the men could decompress before returning to stateside. This was a necessary process that helped the soldiers immensely. As crew members, we loved the layovers in Okinawa primarily for the shopping. We had Japanese seamstress embroidered designs on our garment bags. I had "Coffee Tea or Me" sewn on mine. This cute saying seemed to fit me at that time as a young stewardess.

Our hotel, the Koza Palace, was located downtown in the shopping areas. The hustle and bustle of the city were a stark contrast to the sandy beaches of Hawaii or the calm atmosphere in the Philippines. Okinawa was like stepping back into the 50s era of Japan. The soldiers would hang out in the bar lounge, and if a typhoon was forecast, we were grounded and continued to party. We rarely experienced a real typhoon, thank goodness, but we were fine with our airline's decision.. MAC days were our lifestyle. We were in our own world out there in the Pacific Islands and Asia.

Once our flight pattern took us to Tachikawa, Japan, located in western Tokyo. I remember the retail shops were fantastic, and it was easy to get lost going from one store to another as everything was written in Japanese. However, we were there long enough to make a dent in their local economy.

The Philippines layovers became my favorite. I enjoyed the weather, played tennis in the mornings then spent most of the day at the pool sunbathing. Bloody Mary's followed by breakfast. The Oasis hotel made sure we were well taken care of and prepared American meals in their restaurant. In the evenings, we went to the Officers' club. Several stewardesses found their future husbands during this time. Our American soldiers seemed to be enthralled with us "round eyes" and it was equally as fun to drink and party with them. The Philippines was a plethora of opportunities. Besides the wonderful layovers, we were allowed to co-mat bring back anything, including automobiles in the cargo bins. I brought back a room full of rattan furniture, fan back chairs, and monkey-pod-dishes. If you had the authorization form and there was room in the cargo bins, you could bring it back. This was a fun time and opportunity that was given to us by Continental Airlines. The prices of most things were inexpensive and the shipping was free for crew members. On the longer layovers in the Philippines, many crew members would go into Baguio City to shop or play golf. However, I had heard too many scary incidents and never left the hotel or base areas.

We dated the Air Force, drank with the Army, danced with the Navy, and loved the Marines. Our layovers were filled with romantic dinners, parties, and drinking until eight hours before the next departure. Did we fall in love, yes, many times. I had several serious boyfriends, but one particular handsome man I dated during my two years was an Air Force pilot. Based in the Philippines, he flew in and out of DaNang. I never asked him about his mission, and he never talked about the things he did or saw. We enjoyed one another, and when his tour of duty was over he desired a more permanent relationship, but I was not ready to return to stateside. He would have made a very good husband and father—it's all about timing.

After him, I dated another Air Force officer who had his own cottage bungalow on base. He had a cook and housekeeper, and his place was always immaculate. They left his polished shoes on his steps every morning. There were many cherished rainy nights, and in the evenings, we would sit outside on the enclosed screened porch. It was during this relationship that I started collecting the unused wrapped brownies from the inbound flights along with the milk cartons. Right after our flights, we would take them to wounded soldiers at the hospital on base. We knew if we had told the soldiers on our flights about the brownies and milk, they all would have left them. We wanted them to enjoy their meals because their c-rations would never have fresh milk or brownies. Doing this brought us much joy and allowed us to visit soldiers who had been wounded. My boyfriend always knew my schedule, and when I didn't show up at the hotel, he could find me at the hospital. I enjoyed going from room to room handing out the brownies and milk which lead to conversations with each of them. By the time the van driver dropped us off at the hospital, we had been up nearly seventeen hours, still wearing our hat, gloves, and pearls. Even though we were exhausted, a surge of energy kept us going. Most of their apparent battle injuries, hopefully, healed, but their emotional scars would last a lifetime. These soldiers in the hospital beds were brave to us. We witnessed everything, but the amputees broke our hearts. I vividly still remember one individual soldier. I came across a large room with no door, only a large curtain which kept you from seeing inside the room. With a loud voice, I said, "May I come in?" A voice responded saying, "You may not want to come in?" I replied, "It's ok with me if it's OK with you, there was silence, then I heard, "OK."

As I came around the curtain, my eyes focused on a young mature black man, lying in his bed. His whole right side was open from his wound. He seemed to be a big and strong man, and as I walked closer to him, I just focused on his face and eyes. He smiled despite his condition, and somehow in our brief encounter, we both forgot about where we were. It was moments like these that made our trips to the hospital worth it all. To this day, the memory of that young man remains prominent in my mind.

I have to give thanks to the doctors and nurses at this hospital for their dedicated services. The medical personnel continually received wounded soldiers from the battlefields 24/7. They did amazing surgeries and gave our soldiers the care they needed. I was too young to recognize or thank the doctors and nurses. Without highly professional and dedicated teams of doctors and nurses, no doubt we would have lost far more of our heroes. The hospital is permanently closed today, covered with overgrown bushes and weeds, remnants of its history and the loss of fallen soldiers make it look like a ghost town.

Our dedication to the soldiers, serving them on flights and visiting them in the hospitals were certainly our focus. After returning to my hotel, sleep came easily and mornings came all too quickly. A new fresh day brought about time for 'pampering me' at the beauty shop. Time at the pool and dinners with a special guy or parties at the Officers Club was our lifestyle. Romance was everywhere during our layovers, at debriefing parties, poolside and especially those strolls along Waikiki beaches. The guys didn't have a chance with our crochet bathing suits, wet T-shirt parties, and miniskirts. We were quite young, fun and wild, some more than others. Stewardesses and pilots were always tempted in having romantic interludes. Relationships happened easily while on layovers, especially when you were half way around the world, gone for days, even weeks. Hawaii was Paradise; evenings in the Philippines were warm and tropical, along with their rains. Dinners on the hill of Okinawa were incredibly wonderful. I remember one incident at the Okinawa's Officers' club, their rules and regulations were strict. A pilot friend and I went to the Officers' Club for dinner; I had worn my slacks with a longer blouse. When we entered, they told me that women were not allowed in their restaurant wearing slacks. So, I excused myself, stepped into the restroom and removed my slacks. Miniskirts were popular, and my pink blouse just covered me. They courteously sat us. We chuckled over this most of the evenings. I had to use my napkin to cover my lap.

The MAC flights during those two years had become my life. My times at home were brief, long enough to do laundry and take care of business. In those days, we had two separate phones in our home. One was strictly for Continental scheduling, and the other was for friends and family. The company never knew we had a separate phone line just for them, so if you did not want to fly, you just didn't answer. There were no answering machines or caller ID. This was all good, except when I started dating a crew scheduler, but he was cool and never reported me, even after we broke up.

No matter where we flew, our layovers became party time, from sun up to sundown. We all drank, some more than others. I realized deep down it was an escape from the reality of war as we faced week after week fighting our own anger with the riots and demonstrations back home. Who was right? Who was wrong? We just cared about the soldiers. We were caught in between and kept out of politics. We lived in two different worlds at the same time.

Once we landed at each base in Vietnam, the brave soldiers deplaning bore similar yet stark differences of those soldiers waiting to board. As their boots hit the tarmac, no words were exchanged among them. Some of the men boarding were covered in jungle dirt and faces bearing the burdens they witnessed, still scared and full of raw emotions

Occasionally we would bring back a fallen soldier, and the men would see them placed in the aircraft cargo. My thoughts were, well this is war, and we should expect causalities. Most fallen soldiers were brought back via military aircraft. I quickly had to focus on the men who boarded our aircraft; most had completed their tour, thirteen months or less of physical, mental and emotional battles.

Of the many flights and conversations that took place with thousands of soldiers, the return flights were filled with mixed emotions, some relief, some quiet, some numbness. We let them rest and fed them hot meals. The long flight gave them time to process as they prepared to return to civilian life.

There were two individual soldiers on my flights into Vietnam that I often think about, even to this day. One such young man stopped me in the middle of the aisle to tell me he liked my legs. I have never had anyone tell me anything nice or positive about my bowed legs. Taken back by his comment, I paused in front of him as I looked into his eyes, realizing that he was being sincere. I thanked him and went about my flight duties. Then nearly a year later, this same young man was on my return flight. I remembered him and was happy to see him again, but he immediately shared that most of the men in his unit had been killed. This caused me great sadness, but I held back my tears. As he talked, it was as though part of him was left back on those battlefields. Most of the soldiers on our return flights had lost buddies in their unit.

The second soldier that touched my heart was on a flight over to Nam. I sometimes would take my camera and randomly take pictures of the guys. As I took a picture of several guys, the soldier sitting in the window seat, asked if I would send the photo to his mom. I said, "I would be happy to do that for you." He wrote his mother's name and address, she and I communicated with one another for nearly fifteen years. Her son was quite vivacious, and his mother told me that he came home safely from Vietnam. I was happy to hear that news.

Heading back to the world, the United States was "the world" as opposed to Vietnam, which was not of this world. Always on board we were cheerful, encouraging and sympathetic. After they left our aircraft, the world was not so supportive. The most difficult situations for us were the way our men and women who served in Vietnam were treated when they returned home. As the years and months continued with this war, so did the demonstrations and riots. Our soldiers were told upon their return trips to quickly change into their civilian clothes to avoid confrontation. The exception to this was New York, the people of that great state supported the troops. If protestors tried to discredit a soldier whether carrying a sign or in a demonstration line, the wrath of strong patriots would put a stop to them.

BABY ON BOARD

During my second year of flying the MAC Operation, we only had men on board our flights. The exception occurred on a flight of mine from Hawaii to Travis Air Force Base. She was a petite female civilian who was seven months pregnant. But for some reason, she was allowed to return with us that day. Flying at 35,000 feet, about two hours from landing, her water broke. Thank goodness we had our in-flight manuals. We all were young stewardesses with no knowledge or experience of childbirth. Even though our four-week training was packed with information, the most important tool was our in-flight manuals. We could look up any emergency situation, even childbirth. Rushing to get our manuals, we began our process of preparation according to the instructions. With her water breaking, she then began contractions, so we had to move quickly. We moved the two soldiers who were seated next to her, fixed the three seats with blankets and then tented over the seats to give her privacy. The troops were not even alarmed but joyful to have this happen on their flight home. Some of the items that could be used were things that I carried in my suitcase, the large suitcase which was in the front cargo bin. I rushed to the cockpit asked our 2nd Officer, Moffitt Tinsley, to allow me to climb down the stairs, the hatch was located inside the cockpit. You could lift the hatch and carefully climb down the short stairs. I insisted that I had to get the item myself.

We argued a few minutes but Moffitt was very adamant! I can still hear him saying, "No, BJ, I will get what you need, now tell me what it is that you want."

He then began to tell me that he worked on a ranch and inseminated horses wearing a long, long glove up to his shoulder, so again he said, "I can get whatever you need, now tell me!"

So reluctantly, in front of all three pilots, I said I need my douche bag. I could feel my face turning red, but we were in a tight situation with a baby that could arrive any minute. He got out of his seat and went down, finding my suitcase, he retrieved my red douche bag. Throwing a blanket around it, I then rushed back to our 911 situation.

We did our best following the procedures in the manual and prepared ourselves to deliver a baby. I had never seen such an amazing group of soldiers who gave the mother the support she needed at that critical time. We comforted her, as she continued with contractions. This young girl must have been feeling anxious, but she came to realize in the midst of this ordeal, she had 164 soldiers who were cheering her on.

On approach to Travis Air Force Base, it appeared that the baby was not quite ready to be born. We landed with her in the same position and the two soldiers that we moved, were in different rows on the floor with their backs against the fuselage. After landing, she was whisked off to the hospital. We never did find out if it was a boy or girl, but regardless, the special memories that day were the men on board. They gave her privacy, and as I said earlier, they wanted that baby to be born. After this incident whenever Moffitt and I flew together, there was a twinkle in his eyes as we both smiled remembering that infamous trip.

The baby would be 45 years old today and unaware of 164 soldiers who were ready to be uncles. In today's sophisticated airline industry, there is a professional medical kit on board every aircraft, designed by medical personnel. Also, we can contact a medical facility and speak directly to a physician at the passenger's seat. We have come a long way since the pioneer days of the 60s.

Despite our limitations, however, we offered a supportive environment and did our very best to make the mother safe and comfortable.

Chapter 5

ON BOARD MEMORIES: COFFEE, TEA, AND CONVERSATIONS

We all had our own personal memories of serving and entertaining the troops on board our flights. The laughing and silliness we experienced seemed to bond us together. When I began asking other MAC stewardesses what memories stood out for them, many said they just made sure they had fun. In our own ways, we lightened the atmosphere and created laughter whenever possible. We encouraged those who brought their guitars on board to play. For those who could not sleep, we would play cards or just talk. We could usually tell who needed to talk. Though these flights were routine to us, we were aware of the deep inner changes in the men on their return flights back to the states.

The following paragraphs are recounts from my crew members of a time lost in the pages of history for some but for us only memories. Vietnam fifty plus years ago, we still remember.

Sandi was one of my closest friends from our graduation class. She was a cute, sassy brunette with a good figure, and it did not take her long to find boyfriends. Signing up for the MAC Operations, she confessed she knew nothing about the war or Vietnam, but because I told her to sign up, she did. All she could say was, it was a whirlwind of experiences! She remembers all the shots and flying to unfamiliar countries. Suntans, sunburn, and partying dominated our free time. She became fatigued and admitted she drank way too much. It was difficult flying the troops into Vietnam, but our lifestyle of parties and romantic rendezvous became a diversion—a way to cope with the war.

An awkward situation happened when Sandi met her first love in Okinawa. He was one of the regular soldiers that hung around the bar in the hotel. They had a fling, and she still remembers to this day coming home and being so excited about him, sharing her romantic love for this guy to me, only to find out that we both were dating him. We were crushed but realized all is fair in love and war. To get back at him, I suggested to Sandi that whoever sees him next should inform him that he needed to be checked by a doctor as he had contracted an STD, (sexually transmitted disease). Needless to say, we both stopped seeing him.

Russie had already been flying MAC and was senior to me. She flew two years with the MAC operation before she had to quit due to continual ear infections. She recalls playing games with the soldiers on board our flights. She would buy hundreds of the Bazooka or Double Bubble gum pieces and pack them in her inflight bag. Bubble gum contests were a big hit! Prizes went to those who blew the biggest bubble without it bursting on their face. Spontaneous games and laughter made the going a little easier for us all. We were the entertainment; laughing at us and at each other kept spirits high. Music and guitar playing soothed the nerves so whenever a soldier would bring his guitar on board, we made sure he knew he could play it in between our meal services.

Russie remembers that we experienced mechanical delays periodically, it came with the territory, but she remembers one of her worse mechanical delays happened in Cam Ranh Bay. After landing, the pilots discovered a problem with the brake system and a part that was needed had to be flown in on the next scheduled inbound aircraft. This delay ended up being a nine-hour delay for them in Vietnam. It was in the middle of the night, and we had no power, no lights, and no air conditioning on the airplane. Even with all four cabin doors opened, we were so uncomfortable in the extreme suffocating heat. She shares how tired they all were and desperate to fall off to sleep, even if it was for an hour. We were told we could go to the mess hall, so off we went with pillows and blankets from the airplane. Some of us got up on the tables and slept. We were too tired even to hear the armor vehicles or mortar shooting. We didn't care; we just wanted to sleep, and we could sleep for a few hours before the men on base came in for breakfast. When the repairs had finally been made, they came and woke us up. Can you image what we looked like if the soldiers came into the mess hall for breakfast and saw us beauties on their tables? We looked awful on that return trip, but the guys didn't care; neither did we because the airplane was fixed and we were taking them home. Hoorah! Russie goes on to say that her two years flying the MAC Operations were meaningful, purposeful, and rewarding. Even with the long grueling hours and hot sticky climate, she would not trade that time as she was a true supporter of the troops. Way to go Russie!

Pam was a sharp, cute gal and became a veteran MAC stewardess for four years. When she was a novice, she encountered many memorable events. She shares that at the beginning of the startup program she was green and eager as a new flight attendant. Someone told her MAC was great and therefore she signed up. Call it peer pressure or innocence. She got ALL the shots and wondered where am I going? Vietnam was not on her radar, but that is where the MAC flights would take her.

Flying the troops in and out of the warzone was a bumpy experience and not just the flying. She made the best of her flights, played cards in the wee hours of the night when one or two just couldn't sleep. Little did they know that they were helping her to stay awake. The flights were long, and whenever we could play jokes on the soldiers, it was all in good fun. She once put her apron and wig on a soldier and sent him out in the aisle to serve coffee.

Hearing the men laugh out loud released a lot of tension. The company still required that our hairline be above our collar, so wigs were the popular hairpiece for us gals. Remember, this was the 60s, wigs were worn a lot by us. Pam was in the aisle with trays stacked up on both her arms and a fellow stewardess walked up to her and pulled off the wig she was wearing. She gasped, and the guys were stunned into silence, no doubt embarrassed for her, but when Pam laughed, the atmosphere lightened.

Pam was a fun, loving person who enjoyed life, partied hard, and had a great time on all her flights and layovers. She loved the troops and faced the same challenges that we each faced. She had an infectious laugh and a smile that was as big as her heart. She had many memorable moments and flights that still cause her to be very patriotic, especially when she hears the Star-Spangled Banner. She would say, those troops taught her that serving was a duty. Yes, she played hard, and fell in love just like the rest of us, even with the married pilot who wanted to take me to the movie in Hawaii. He became "the pilot" for many of us. Because Pam loved to play jokes on anyone that was vulnerable, she has her favorite story of long ago. On one of her layovers, she and another stewardess, along with "the pilot" wanted to play a joke on another pilot. They stripped down to their underwear, got under the covers and made a phone call to the other pilot. When he knocked on the door, they said come on in. As he observed the situation, they invited him to join them. He began undressing but not all the way as they threw the covers off, and he then realized it was a joke. The glue that held us together to make the most of those MAC days was our camaraderie—laughter and jokes, along with interludes of romances.

We all experienced mechanicals; flying with three engines was not an unusual occurrence. We would be halfway across the Pacific, and our pilots would have to shut down one of our four engines due to a malfunction. They never worried. It was just a matter of fact that would occur every now and then. Remember we still had three engines remaining. If our pilots weren't worried, neither were we. Severe mechanicals could cause us delays, sometimes days, as parts had to be flown in. Thus our aircraft were grounded, and you hoped the country where you were grounded was somewhat civilized or safe. Diversions were sometimes welcome, especially in Bangkok even though it was extremely hot and humid. We loved the opportunity to eat and possibly shop. Remember this was the sixties; the airport was very small with a restaurant upstairs and windows opened to catch any breeze because there was no air conditioning. The shopping was slim, but occasionally, we could purchase some jade pieces and have them made into a ring or necklace, expensive in today's market.

We were so proud and thankful when the guys returned home on our flights. Overall, we didn't joke with them on those flights. We fed them, and they quickly fell off to sleep. The returning soldiers were thankful to be able to leave Vietnam alive. When the wheels retracted into the fuselage, the applause was heard throughout the cabin. The applause reached the cockpit causing the pilots to smile.

I remembered an incident that happened after I returned to domestic flying. A male passenger was asleep and laying down on all three seats. We were getting ready to land, and all passengers had to be in an upright position with their seatbelt fastened. Because I had just returned from flying MAC, what happened next did not alarm or scare me. I had leaned in to tap him on the shoulder, and he woke up with such a fearful reaction, for a split second, I think he thought he was in Nam? He quickly raised his arm to grab my throat, I knew immediately he was a veteran, I whispered, "It's OK, it's OK, and you are all right." He calmed down and apologized to me. I recognized what trauma can do to a person, and I think by my reassuring him, made a huge difference with him. Grief and trauma can accompany major events in our lives. War can bring about painful emotional experiences, accompanied with sorrow and fear. Trauma can affect us in many ways. Freedom is never free.

Pat W. was a notorious prankster. She got away with a lot of practical jokes and could do things that none of us could ever do without getting fired or reprimanded. She was a fun person on layovers and on our flights. One outrageous event happened on a flight out of Vietnam. The ground personnel was ready to begin boarding, and just before they began, the Captain needed to use the forward lavatory. As the soldiers boarded the aircraft, Pat unlocked the lavatory door and swung it open. There was the Captain sitting on the toilet with his pants down; she began introducing the soldiers to their Captain. The startled look from the Captain as well as the soldiers remained the high point of hilarity on that flight and one of the memories we all retold.

Stewardess Billie Jo shared a very memorable moment while flying her MAC flight. She too had experienced the fun flights with jokes and games. However, she remembers her first Christmas while being away from home and on a layover. Our crew members were melancholic and felt sad being away from our families. There were no Christmas lights anywhere, and we didn't feel like having a party. We tried to make the best of it despite our feelings. We got together in one of our rooms when a knock came at the door. Our Captain, Don Ballard brought in a Christmas tree with decorations. We lit up, and that tree changed the whole atmosphere.

There were similar stories we heard from soldiers, telling us what they would do to make it possible to have a Christmas tree. We should never take our holidays for granted, for they are special to us, something we learn to cherish, especially when we are out of the country.

FYI: Back in 60s every aircraft had a Bible on board donated by the Gideon's Foundation, as the years passed, they began to be removed. However, the aircraft that are equipped with over water rafts do include a Bible in the emergency equipment.

OUR CONTINENTAL PILOTS

As stewardesses, we had our experiences with the passengers, but the pilots certainly had their own stories. Due to military routes, our airline, headed by Maverick owner, Robert F. Six and his wife Audrey Meadows, experienced a fast growth spurt. He ran the airlines while she chose our uniform designs and colors. Most of our pilots came straight out of the military after completing their 2,000 flight hours. Unreservedly, our pilots were awesome, as we witnessed landings and take-offs in the remote unconventional area of the MAC operations. It was a Maverick Airline filled with incredible stories. The captains had full authority to make the MAC flights successful and safe.

Our Boeing 707s had three pilots, captain, first officer and the second officer. The second officer handled the fuel consumption as well as cabin temperature. Back in those days, the second officer recorded our names in a flight log, inadequate for today's computer age, where aircraft can land themselves without the assistance of pilots. Nevertheless,

I was impressed with the flight crew's abilities to fly our aircraft. They loved being pilots as much as we loved being stewardesses. I could distinguish the landings, whether it was Navy or Air Force pilot. Yes, I could tell the difference. Air Force landings were smoother compared to the ruff landings by the Navy pilots.

Flying the long MAC flights gave us the opportunities to visit them in the flight deck. On domestic flights, there was no time, other than taking them a beverage or meal. I loved watching their piloting skills, which included calculating our miles and using the control panel. Flying and landing aircraft takes exceptional skills. Fascinated with all the controls on the panel, I asked a million questions. They had aviation charts and aeronautical flight maps showing the road maps in the sky. Most of our pilots were fairly young, ranging from 25 up to their 30s. We did have the youngest pilots in the industry because of our growth.

Our pilots were calm and methodical in the flight deck. On those long flights, they enjoyed our company as they were not allowed to fall asleep. We would joke, laugh and learn about one another. I loved going up into the flight deck during the middle of the night, looking out the windows seeing the moon at 32,000 feet. I enjoyed a peaceful moment, the silence only broken by the humming sounds of the engines.

Pilots needed strength and stamina piloting across the Pacific and then into Vietnam. Flying these soldiers out of Vietnam, made those long flights worth it. Laughter and jokes filled much of our time. I mentioned how humid the weather was in Vietnam. Well, I decided to play a joke on our pilots. I had worn my bathing suit under my dress. Perspiration and sweat always ran down our dresses while we sat on our jump seats. It couldn't be helped; we just lived with it.

However, on this flight after takeoff, I went up to the cockpit and said, "I can't take this heat anymore, and I am taking my dress off."

Well, all three heads turned and watched in amazement as I unzipped my dress, quickly pulling it off and then breaking out in laughter. I am not a jokster but sure enjoyed this opportunity to make the pilots laugh.

Yes, we had a lot of great pilots, some stood out more than others. I only fell in love with one pilot, the one who wanted to take me to the movie in Hawaii. He had my heart for many years.

Though we had times of levity, each month that passed brought about a routine that was not so joyful. I am not sure when the realization of this war began to leave an impact on me. Many platoons that we took over came back with less than half who survived. I began asking when will this war end? Yes, we had our moments of laughter, but those days seemed to wane as the war waged on.

Chapter 6

SECOND GLANCE ...
SECOND CHANCE

Two of my co-workers became co-partners, from "Hi, how are you?" to saying "I do," 27 years later. God always says, "He gives us hope and a future." The following is based on a true love story.

Not all pilots fell to the lifestyle or temptation; some remained faithful. One was Tom Schuchat, one of our second officers. They recorded our names in the flight manual, kept the cabin temperature the way we like it, and most importantly kept tabs on the fuel in all four engines. Most second officers were cheerful and lightened the atmosphere of our long flights. Tom was one of those pilots whose sense of humor, intelligence and laughter created a fun trip. He was a regular guy, kidded, but didn't flirt and always treated us with respect.

Tom's career began in college as AF ROTC where he learned how to fly. He served in the Air Force and was stationed in Saigon from 1965 to 1966 where his crew supplied the bases with ammunition. While on a layover at Clark Air Force Base in the Philippines, he went to the Officers Club where he ended up talking to one of the Continental pilots, who encouraged him to apply with Continental after the end of his tour. God puts us in the right places at the right time. He was hired in 1966 and soon found himself back in Vietnam with Continental Airlines as a second officer. Instead of transporting ammunition, he now was transporting the troops on a commercial airline. He was quite familiar with the terrain of Vietnam and was an asset to Continental on these routes. Because of our growth, the pilots moved quite quickly up to their next position. He flew only eleven months as a second officer, then moved to the right seat to be a first officer and later when he returned to the domestic routes, was promoted to captain. He had a long career with Continental and finally retired in 1995.

As he began his military career, Penny was building her career as well. A tall, beautiful blonde, full of life and adventure, her bubbly personality captured many hearts. Only having flown a short time when she turned twenty-one, she flew the Military MAC Operations in 1964. On her very first flight and layover in Hawaii where the layovers would easily be three days on the beaches of Waikiki, her lily-white skin had not been exposed to the sun. She was told to use baby oil and add iodine to get a good tan. While lying on the beach, drinking coconut cocktails, she suffered a severe and painful sunburn. She barely could make it across the waters to her next layover. She can laugh today about that memory, remembering how naïve she was in those days.

When asked about her years flying the Military MAC Operations, she would share her sadness about how the troops were treated when they came home. We all felt this pain, and maybe that added to our drinking on layovers? "Damn this war," she would say. She vividly remembers a landing in Saigon where the bombings caused their crew to run to the bunkers. Penny was always fashionable with her Continental uniform, high heels, pearls, hat, and white gloves. Dressed for the runways of New York style, she was found with the other crew members running quickly to the bunkers in the hottest, humid weather conditions. Sweat began to run down her whole body—her make-up destroyed. Once inside, they ran from one room to another to get to safety. She finally found a place to sit down in a corner and from exhaustion despite the danger and sounds, fell off to sleep. Her crew members never let her forget that snooze while bombs fell nearby.

We shared special memories as all of us would leave the airbases in Vietnam, hearing the soldiers always applaud when the wheels went up on takeoff. When the troops boarded the airplane, we soon learned that some just came out of the battlefields. Whenever their language would get strong, Penny, who was only a couple of years older, would remind them that there were ladies on board. She also made many trips to the hospital in the Philippines, no matter how tired she was to bring leftover brownies and milk to our guys.

As crew members, Penny and Tom remember the long flights, fun layovers, dinners, and parties. They were co-workers and even ate dinners with other crew members at the Koza Palace in Okinawa. They never looked at one another with romantic interest. Tom was married with a commitment that was respected and admired. As time passed and lives changed, Penny married, and seven years later went through a divorce. Tom's life also changed, as he too had divorced. Neither one knew about the other.

Then in 1992, on Christmas Eve at Houston International Airport, they both had just finished their individual flights. While walking through the terminal, they saw one another after many years from those Vietnam days. They stopped and briefly talked, having a twinkle in their eyes for one another. Penny remembers looking at Tom's sexy smile and thought to herself how handsome he looked to her.

Tom asked, "Still married?" Penny responded, "No," and he said, "Neither am I." She needed to leave right away and catch her communing flight. He asked if he could call her and she responded, yes! As she walked away, he shouted, "What is your number?"

She shouted it back, and the calls and courting led them to a second chance romance. In 1995 with a few friends, they flew to Las Vegas and were married in the Elvis Presley Chapel. There were no more Heartbreak Hotels and no more, "Are you lonesome tonight?" Becoming Tom's co-pilot for life, Penny and Tom shared an incredible life story. They weathered their turbulent years with parents who lived with them but continued to draw many of their airline friends together, sharing love, life, and laughter. Their home became filled with many accomplishments, but most importantly, the love they shared for one another, family, friends, and their many happy puppy dogs.

Both retired, Penny hung her wings in 2013. She was told by her friends when she started flying that she would only last six months but proved them wrong after her career with Continental Airlines of 49 years. Traveling the world, with the airlines and with one another, they have lifetime memories.

Early in 2013, Tom succumbed to fast-growing cancer and passed away March 25, 2013. Penny to this day loves to quote, "Don't cry because it's over, smile because it happened." She loved that Second Glance and Second Chance that changed their lives forever.

Chapter 7

THE PRICE OF PEACE

It is the Soldier who salutes the flag, who serves beneath the flag and whose coffin is draped by the flag. May we never forget those we have lost and those left behind.

Statistic showed the price of this war. America lost over 58,000 lives, 1600 missing in action, and over 700 prisoners of war. Courage defined is the ability to do something that frightens you and strength in the face of pain and grief.

I sensed the fear and concerns on my flights while taking them over to Vietnam and witnessed their pain and grief when they returned to stateside. The reflections of the war were evident on their faces. The price of peace is difficult to measure. Less we forget the thousands of walking wounded who still fight today with the effects of PTSD.

"My husband and I, along with hundreds of thousands wore our MIA bracelets for a very long time. We both cried when we saw their names on the Wall. We removed them from our wrist and placed them in a memorial cubicle box in our home."

Lt. Colonel Robert Barnett 10-3-67
CM/Sgt. Dean A Duvall USAF 13 Mar 66 SVN

"What we once enjoyed and deeply loved, we can never lose for all that we love deeply became a part of us."
Helen Keller

WE REMEMBER

Memorial Day
5.24.15

We remember the day
When the pain gave way
To the bright little bundle
Which awed us to wonder

What one day you would become
A beautiful daughter, a handsome son
There's no way in the beginning to know
The way you would go
A doctor, a lawyer, a teacher
An engineer, a scientist, a preacher

But you made a choice; you had a voice
A soldier you would become
You laughed; you cried
During Basic Training thought you died

You donned the uniform of one who would conform
to orders and commands
You were taught to take a stand
A stand you took for me and others you would never meet
Then you made the ultimate sacrifice
You laid down your life

Today as we remember
Our hearts are truly tender
Thank you for the sacrifice
Of laying down your precious life

Freedom is never free
Your sacrifice guaranteed that for me
To our fallen heroes—may you rest in peace
We remember your sacrifice to this Nation
Because freedom is never free.

God Bless You and God Bless America

Author and Pastor Ricky Texada,
My Breaking Point, God's Turning Point
Covenant Church, Colleyville, Texas

HANOI "HILTON" HEROES
COMMANDER PAUL GALANTI
US NAVY RETIRED

Paul Galanti went from US Navy Pilot to POW for seven years at the infamous Hanoi Hilton. His photo appeared on the Life magazine cover Oct. 1967 sitting on a bench that they brought in for him during a propaganda photo shoot as he displayed his middle fingers between his knees. He doesn't reflect on the years he lost, but focuses on today, being the best time in his life.

He reflects, "Although I lost more than seven years, I feel that this present life and time are my best years. No day is a bad day when there is a door knob on the inside of the door." Easy to see why he is called the "attitude adjuster" by many.

Born into a military family, Paul experienced many countries over his growing up years. In 1962 he entered the Naval Academy and then into jet training. Aboard the carrier USS HANCOCK, he headed to Southeast Asia in 1965. Lieutenant Commander Galanti flew 97 combat missions before being shot down June 17, 1966, and finally released February 12, 1973. Surviving the atrocities and torture of war gave him a special appreciation for life.

This is an account of his experience reported in *We Came Home* by Captain and Mrs. Frederick A. Wyatt and Barbara Powers Wyatt (P.O.W Publications, 1977).

"My nearly seven years of captivity could be summed up in the space of a postage stamp. But I learned a valuable lesson in appreciation."

The years of zero (which he does not count) in Commander Galanti's life began when he was shot down on June 17, 1966, near Vinh, North Vietnam. His A-4 Skyhawk was hit after an attack on a railroad siding and, although he could see the rescue destroyer off-shore, his plane went out of control before he could reach them.

He ejected from his plane, was captured, taken north to Hanoi, and paraded in the infamous "Hanoi March." "This was ostensibly a spontaneous demonstration on the part of the Vietnamese," says Galanti. "However, as we left the park, the blindfolds were removed, we were handcuffed in pairs, and marched into the street. The first thing I saw was a bunch of political cadres with megaphones inciting the people. At the end of the first block, there was a big truck with movie equipment in it to play this spectacle up. A man came running up from the side, gave me a soccer-like kick in the groin, and I went down in a heap. There was so much yelling it sounded like Notre Dame scoring a touchdown at South Bend. It lasted about forty-five minutes. They finally got us to a soccer stadium where they had trucks waiting, then took us back to the prison."

In addition to the physical tortures, Commander Galanti was subjected to an agonizing session after "violating the prison regulations." Having received two letters and a package from Phyllis, his wife, he assumed it was a special deal to make him look bad in the eyes of his fellow POWs. In order to show that such was not the case, he threw a package of Lifesavers to one of the other cells in the bathhouse. A guard saw and reported it. For this, he was made to sit on a small stool in an interrogation room during the coldest part of the year. He sat there for ten days and nights, drugged and deprived of sleep, before being forced to apologize to the camp commander.

Although these and other individual torture stories often seemed the result of individual North Vietnamese actions,

Galanti warns Americans not to forget the overall goal of communism is world domination. "It often got blackest just after they started smiling," he says.

America will always be indebted to patriots like Paul Galanti who represents what the US stands for—Freedom. God Bless Paul and all those who suffered for our country.

COLONEL SAM JOHNSON
USAF DECORATED WAR HERO
AND DISTINGUISHED STATESMAN

Sam Johnson, a decorated war hero, and native Texan ranks among the few members of Congress to fight in combat. During his 29-year career in the U.S. Air Force, Col. Johnson flew combat missions in both the Korean and Vietnam Wars. He endured nearly seven years as a Prisoner of War in Hanoi, including 42 months in solitary confinement. Following his distinguished military career, Col. Johnson established a home-building business in North Dallas from scratch and serves in the Texas State legislature.

Sam Johnson was introduced to us at the Vietnam War Commemoration as Texas Congressman Sam Johnson. He was a Colonel in the USAF. It was a special honor to all those present, military men and women, the press and those of us who were invited to this special commemoration. His introduction brought a standing ovation with applause that deafened your ears.

His tall stature along with his strong stance took center stage. His walk seemed hindered by some awkwardness, maybe stiffness that comes with age or from the damage incurred from being a Prisoner of War victim. We were told his back had been broken and he suffered torture and solitary confinement for months. His smile was broad, and his facial appearances seemed gentle. When he began to speak, there was no doubt about his strength and vigor that came forth. He immediately made us feel comfortable as he began to give us statics about the war in Vietnam. 91% glad they served, 74% would serve again, ½ of 1% were charged with crimes, 9% discharged, 80% adjusted to civilian life, 85% of Americans today give honor and gratitude.

He told us of his continual involvement with other vets, especially at hospitals, and had been instrumental in the development of two new clinics for Vets in Plano, Texas. He commented and paused to say, "Vets love Freedom and Democracy."

"I worked for General Westmoreland, and I served two tours. While in combat, I was shot down, captured and spent nearly seven years as a POW. It was hell here on earth. There were 11 of us, and we communicated through the walls using the 'tap code.' I was labeled hard-core. Their defense was to make us think we were isolated and alone. I was sent to solitary confinement with my legs in shackles with no light for 42 months. It was during these months where God helped me to survive. I prayed just to be able to see daylight. There was a hurricane that came through filling my cell with three feet of water. They unlocked our shackles, because of the force of the hurricane, some timbers were pulled away in my cell and for the first time in months, I saw light.

I spent 74 days with my legs in stock. I learned how to kill flies but thought I was going to die every day ... It was the deepest time of my life, and that is where I learned to pray like never before. I had this incredible peace and hope. I was released after nearly seven years and came home in 1975. I came to realize that we each have a purpose in life, sometimes we have to make decisions to forget or let go, often many times in a day. America was not the same when

I returned home. Veterans were not treated well. I chose to serve in government, to support Veterans and educate our youth, especially about patriotism. Events like this one today remind us "Freedom is not Free, there is a cost, especially with those who lost their lives."

Colonel Johnson was awarded two Silver Stars, two Legions of Merit, Distinguished Flying Cross, one Bronze Star with Valor, two Purple Hearts, four Air Medals and three Outstanding Unit Awards. He has served as U.S. Representative for the Texas 3rd district since 1991.

Thank you for your service and love of country. God has used you mightily, and we thank God for you and all our POW's.

The Lord is my shepherd,
I shall not be in want.
He makes me lie down in green pastures,
he leads me beside quiet waters,
he restores my soul.
He guides me in paths of righteousness for his name's
sake. Even though I walk through the valley
of the shadow of death,
I will fear no evil,
for you are with me;
your rod and your staff,
they comfort me.
You prepare a table before me
in the presence of my enemies.
You anoint my head with oil;
my cup overflows.
Surely goodness and love will follow me
all the days of my life,
and I will dwell in the house of the Lord forever.

Psalm 23

Chapter Eight

HIGH SCHOOL HEROES
CLASS OF 1962

From the football field of Hawthorne High to the battlefields of Vietnam, these football players led our school to many championship games. They were tested to the limits fighting to win each game; little did these seniors know that their teamwork and skills would play out in the real-life war drama in Vietnam. There were other male students who also went to Vietnam from our high school; I am sorry I did not know them. Some lost their lives, and I wish to thank their families for raising honorable men. Each of the following men served in the US Military to defend an unknown country in an unknown land. Air Force and Army became their insignia and uniform. These heroes were mine, but they could have been from your high school. Thank you, Dan, David, Jim and George.

HAWTHORNE HIGH SCHOOL, HAWTHORNE, CALIFORNIA

Dan Dye   David Stark
Jim Reale   George Rea

DAN DYE, ARMY
NO TEARS IN NAM
1968

The 60s era had exploded into emotional turmoil with the hippie movement and the Vietnam War. When young men and women enlisted or were drafted out of high school, they soon faced a revolution against the establishment and faced an unpopular war. Our American society was becoming divided, we had the "Make Peace, Not War" movement, versus those who were willing to fight and serve in our military. It was a sad time in history when our soldiers were shown much disrespect—hatred; they were even spat upon when they returned home. Forgive us, Lord! Forgive us Vietnam Veterans. With all respect, I honor and dedicate my chapters to the high school heroes who served in Vietnam. Lest we should forget that over 56,000+ lost their lives. These were soldiers who died for the cause of freedom. Every soldier MADE a difference every soldier MAKES a difference!

My next story is about a star high school football player and track team athlete who holds the Hawthorne High shot put record that was set 52 years ago. Dan Dye graduated from Hawthorne High School in California, class of 1962. Dan was born April 5, 1944. In high school Dye was the starting defensive tackle and offensive center and competed on the track team. He earned seven varsity letters. After high school, he attended El Camino College where he continued to excel and was a champion of the shot put and still holds local and national records.

After graduation, Dan started working at North American Aviation. In 1967 he married and in the same year was drafted into the US Army. During his military training, his wife was expecting their first child. He was stationed at Fort Ord, California for basic training, where the barracks were kept at 56 degrees because of a meningitis outbreak. Dye was then stationed at Ft. Polk Louisiana for advanced infantry training, then on to Ft. Benning, Georgia for non-commissioned officer training, earning the rank of E-5 Sergeant within nine months in the military. Graduating from Ft. Benning, he was then stationed at Fort Lewis, Washington for OJT (on the job training) with a new basic training unit.

In 1968, Dan was sent to the Republic of Vietnam. He honestly believed he would never make it back from Vietnam. Sergeant Dye was the assigned Squad Leader for a grunt (infantry) unit. At the age of 24, Dye earned the title "Old Man" because most of the drafted soldiers were only 18 or 19 years old. At the end of his Vietnam tour Dye was performing as Platoon Sergeant. However, he wasn't given the rank or paid at the E-7 level. Dan remembers his flight on Continental Airlines MAC flight in 1968. He recalls each stopover, first to Hawaii, Guam, Philippines, and final stop the Republic of Vietnam. At each stopover, they could deplane to smoke and stretch their legs while the aircraft was being cleaned and catered. Dye didn't smoke so he spent the time writing his wife a letter and begins to experience the changes in weather and scenery.

Easter Sunday morning, March 1968, this high school all-American football player, shot putter, and expecting father, landed in the Republic of Vietnam, a dawning of a new way of life for Sergeant Dan Dye. He knew his Lord and Savior was on his side and was ready to face the insurmountable danger.

On arriving in Vietnam, Sergeant Dye boarded a school bus with chain link fencing over the glassless windows to protect from hand grenades being thrown into the bus, an indication of what lay ahead. Traveling without weapons through a thick, dense jungle on winding roads, while rockets, small-armed rifle fire, and mortars were going off all around them, gave everyone an uneasy and vulnerable feeling. He then arrived at Bien Hoa, a distribution supply station for replacing units in the field that had lost troops in combat.

Sergeant Dye wasn't issued his weapons and ammunition until he arrived at his unit in the Americal Division (23rd Infantry Division) on Firebase Sue. His backpack weighed over 80 pounds. Members of his platoon advised him that this "real warzone" was nothing like any training he had back in "the World," the USA. (Vietnam was called Hell, and the United States was the World). The perpetual, unrelenting heat and humidity made it necessary to shed most of their heavy backpack equipment and only keep the bare necessities, like one shirt, one pair of pants (the ones you were wearing), two sets of socks, one set of boots, wash cloth, one towel which was used as a sweat rag, pillow, padding for the rucksack (backpack), plus ammunition, hand grenades, medical supplies, mosquito repellent, pen and paper for writing letters, and helmet. Within the first three months, he lost 30 pounds living and fighting in the jungle, eating only one C-ration per day for weeks at a time. He was never stationed at a base but went from one mission to another. Mail Call letters to and from home were the highlight of the day.

He began telling me of the black pajamas the Vietnamese wore. Black pajamas were worn by the men, women, and children, as well as being the uniform of the Viet Cong from the North and the South. The North Vietnamese soldiers wore olive green uniforms. There were several cultural differences between them; the North Viet Cong were influenced and financed by the communists. The South Vietnamese Army fought against the communist regime for their freedom and their land. The communists wanted to present the "revolution" as a Southern movement. The black pajamas were part of this propaganda. It made it difficult for our soldiers to distinguish the real enemy, which played into the communist ploy, that we were the enemy.

There were times when Vietnamese soldiers would change sides in the middle of a battle, the "Chu Hoys" (slang for surrender). These were Vietnamese soldiers that were fighting for the North, who when captured, requested to fight for the South and with the US troops.

As stewardesses, we also could not identify the enemies either, and after the soldiers deplaned, we cleaned our aircraft, never risking an enemy on board.

In Dan's encounters in the jungles, the men reminded themselves this is war, and there are no tears in Nam. He recalls the numerous incidents when he truly should have been wounded or killed. Each time he was called on a mission or sent to another firebase, his platoon was attacked and incurred causalities. Replacement sergeants would also be wounded or killed. The men would say, "it don't mean Nut-in'," as a way of coping. Sometimes Dan could mourn, meaning to feel bad or more accurately to think, "I am glad it wasn't me" or "why him and not me?" An hour after a soldier was killed, it was no longer talked about, but to survive, the saying "it don't mean Nut-in" had to become stronger than their emotions. They soon learned that short timers, those with less than two months until they rotated back home to the World, were often careless, many lost their lives weeks or days before they were scheduled to go back to the World. He said many of the new incoming troops were killed within the first week of being in Vietnam.

Always on watch and being very careful, Dan remembers a jungle mission when he was "getting short" (getting close to going back to the World) he received rifle fire from a sniper. All his anger, frustration and killer instincts surfaced. He dropped his pack, taking only his weapon and ammunition and began to run after the sniper. Living in the jungle taught him the tricks of the enemy, which at that moment dissipated. As he pursued the sniper, his adrenaline pushed him further into the jungle without his platoon's support. As he was running, he ran across a log bridge over a body of water. Half way across the bridge he saw a snake. Seeing that snake immediately snapped him out of his rage. However, he could not stop his momentum on the log without falling into the water where there were possibly more water moccasin snakes. Dan jumped over the snake and ran to the other side of the stream and realized his mistake. He took up a firing position and waited for his platoon. Safe, yet emotionally and physically exhausted, he pushed ahead to the next mission.

Dan's unit had many missions; another was to clear the brick buildings that were built and left by the French army. The North Vietcong would leave heroin in large stockpiles for their men to use before they went into battle. So our soldiers fought against crazy men who were high on heroin. Hazardous fighting, land mines and booby traps littered the treacherous paths, so they did not walk on trails; they walked through the middle of rice paddies or cut their way through the jungle. In another incident that almost took his life, Dan's platoon was clearing a village when a land mine blew up, killing a Vietnamese man that was leading them through his village, leaving Dan's entire squad struck by fragments of the mine. The Vietnamese man, who was just two people ahead of Dan, had tripped the land mine and it killed him instantly. Several of the squad members were evacuated due to their wounds and never returned to the field. Dan was awarded a Purple Heart due to his wounds, again wondering why his life was spared.

The North Vietcong had several booby traps that killed or maimed. One was called, "Bouncing Betty." When soldiers would step on a Bouncing Betty, it would pop up and explode three feet in the air, wounding whoever it hit. It took two soldiers to carry the wounded and bleeding soldier to safety. The North Vietcong knew that it took out three soldiers from the battle. Another hazard the men had to keep watch for were the Pongee Pits. They were pits lined with sharp bamboo spikes. The object was to impale the soldier when he stepped into the pit. It sounded horrid, and it was a horrible death. Then there were the "spider holes," a camouflaged hole dug in the ground large enough for one Viet Cong soldier to hide. He would pop up, fire a weapon or throw a hand grenade, then drop back into the spider hole to again camouflage himself and try to disappear.

There were numerous booby traps that killed our men. The Viet Cong traps unfortunately at times took out village children while they played innocently along the roadsides or close to town. Unfortunately for our men even children, wearing black pajamas would throw grenades at them and then run.

Dan said that it was not unusual to see young boys nine to eleven years old carrying rifles. He remembers one day some local children were playing in concertina wire, a mine was tripped and exploded, blowing a child 20 feet into the air. The lifeless body laid on the ground as a crying mother ran to the child. Dan remembered the mother looking at the American soldiers, expecting them to put her son back together. These vivid memories are difficult to shake off and sometimes trigger other events that haunt soldiers.

While on a routine search and destroy mission, his unit searched a small village that was suspected of harboring enemy troops. After searching the village and appearing to be safe, they spent time there for the remainder of the day. They gave out some c-rations, tried to make friends with the village people, and even took pictures of their primitive living conditions. When the sun was starting to set, Dan's unit moved out and secured an NDP (night defensive position). One of the first routine things they always did, was to call in artillery strikes. They started by having the artillery battery fire a marking round, which was only a smoke round. They called in a location away from their position and the village. The purpose was to be able to call in fire support in the event they were under attack during the night. From the marking round, they would radio in the next rounds to a location where they thought would be the most likely position of attack. Then they would adjust the location of the artillery rounds by radio. One of their major problems were the outdated maps. Things were old and had changed. On this night when the marking round landed, it was short of where we intended for it to land. It fell into the village that they had just left. A few minutes later the village people started walking in a line toward our NDP wailing, carrying a small child that our marking round had struck in the head, severing the top two inches of the child's head off. The villagers wanted the great GI's medic to reattach the severed head back to the lifeless child. Dan realized he had taken pictures of that child just hours before this tragic event and they couldn't let the villagers into their perimeter for security reasons. They always were careful not to shoot innocent villagers, but accidents like this happened.

Meanwhile, back in the states, Dan's baby boy was born on October 21. Another intervention for Dan happened December 21, 1968. Dan's baby son required emergency surgery. The doctor and his wife requested the Army to allow him to come home on an emergency leave to be by his baby's side during the operation; however, Dan didn't get back to see his son until after the surgery. The trip back to the World may have saved Dan's life because his platoon and the entire company lost 75% of their unit, wiped out in a battlefield. It was a tragic day for our military, as the losses were high. Dan felt had he been there; he too would have been killed. His life continued to be spared.

After returning to the states on the emergency leave, it was determined he did not have to return to Vietnam because he was a short timer and his Army tour soon ended. His transition back home was not easy; their baby's surgery was successful, but his marriage was not. Dan is known as a gentle man, and he survived an incredible war. His life in Vietnam depended upon his skills and marksmanship and his faith. Making the changes from the jungles of Vietnam to city and family life was difficult. He made it, yet our society treated him with no respect on his return home, and now he faced a rocky marriage.

He decided to finish his college education and pursue a career in law enforcement as a police officer. While taking Police Science courses, one of his instructors was the Chief of Police in the city of El Segundo. His instructor encouraged him to join the El Segundo Police Department; however, he had his eye set on working for Los Angeles Police Department. With an athletic build, 6'3" weighing 235 pounds with only ten percent body fat; he was rejected by LAPD who determined he should not weigh over 201 pounds. He was told by them not even to bother applying until his weight was less than 201 pounds. He then interviewed for the Police Department in El Segundo. During a very long and arduous interview by a stern ex-Marine police sergeant, Dan thought, he would not pass the interview and wouldn't be getting the job. During the interview, the ex-Marine discovered Dan had served in Vietnam, and he was hired and started the police academy one week later.

During this intense and stressful training, Dan came home from a day at the police academy and found a note from his wife saying, "I am gone, don't look for me."

She left him taking their son and the car he had purchased prior to meeting her, leaving him without transportation. Dan felt the emotional overload, but pushed through and graduated with high honors.

Dan overcame many obstacles to face a hopeful future. The entry-level job for El Segundo Police Department was on patrol, which he did for seven years, and then he was assigned to ride motorcycles in the traffic division, where he served for nearly seventeen years. Dan then found himself facing a different kind of combat. The final chapter of his Police career found him on the elite SWAT team. His military experience had prepared him with the skills for being what he calls the "Door Man." The ram- carrier was the first man at the door carrying an eighty-pound ram to crash doors in if the suspects refused to open the door after the announcement: "Police officers! We have a search warrant! Open the door!" He later became the team leader and led the SWAT team to gain entry into many undesirable and dangerous locations.

Dan retired from the police force after twenty-five years. However, he is continuing to serve and safeguard his fellow man in executive protection.

We honor you, Dan, thank you for your service in Vietnam and society. God Bless you.

For further information on Dan Dye's police career and SWAT team activities, refer to the book, Frangible Quest by Rex Fowler.

"Have I not commanded you? Be strong and courageous. Do not be terrified; do not be discouraged, for the Lord your God will be with you wherever you go."
Joshua 1:9

DAVID STARK
U.S. AIR FORCE SERGEANT
VIETNAM 1967-68

A hero from high school to Vietnam to becoming a Firefighter, what do heroes look like? They are distinguished by courage, admired for brave deeds and noble qualities. Our hero's come in all kinds of shapes and sizes. These are the men and women who serve in our Military Armed Forces, from high school to college ages, some older. They are young and full of life, eager to serve, united by one bond, "courage." Courage defined by Webster's dictionary, "the attitude of facing and dealing with anything recognized as dangerous, difficult or painful, instead of withdrawing from it, fearless or brave; valor."

It is an awesome sight and a proud moment whenever we see our military in uniform. As I began to interview this next Vietnam Veteran and former Fireman, there is a thread of camaraderie that continues not only in soldiers but also among the brotherhood of Firefighters and Police Officers. It's a bond that is indescribable, strong enough that no force can break.

Our 9/11 was a horrific, catastrophic event of unbelievable proportions. Vietnam Veteran and Firefighter, David Stark had the urgency in his heart to get to New York.

*"The wise heart will know the proper time
and the just way."*
Ecclesiastes 8:5

It was his time again, to come to the aid of his fellow Firefighters in New York. All his years as an ex-military and firefighter surged up in him. Men and women from all over

America came to the aid of our country. David responded immediately; this was a true measure of his character. This trip was possible through his superior at his fire station. He paid for his own airline ticket, flew from Los Angeles to New York and spent ten days in the dangerous rubble, breathing all those ashes as they searched for bodies. He did it without reward or fame; this is what a hero looks like. David Stark was born July 27, 1944, raised in a Christian home, and attended Church as he grew up. After graduating from Hawthorne, he attended El Camino Jr. College. His upbringing and physical build allowed him to play sports while growing up. He was an outstanding football player at our high school and actively involved with the school's House of Representatives. After interning as a fireman, David joined the Air Force in 1967.

Boot camp was intense, and he vividly remembers the inoculation shots that covered every type of disease. As he jokingly says, "let's not forget, all those inoculation shots that covered every type of disease known to man." His specific training included intelligence information and civil engineering training, thus he was given the rank of Sergeant. His athletic abilities surged while in training, and he received the highest marks for military skills from his commanding officers.

After the completion of his civil engineering training, David was given the rank of Sergeant. His orders to Vietnam landed him at Cam Ranh Bay, November 1967, a date he says he will always remember. He did not question that his life would be lost but only saw himself as a defender and soldier with the utmost calling, serving in the United States Air Force. It was his faith that carried him across the Pacific, giving him peace and stability in all that he would be facing in Vietnam. He remembers that the flight took 17 long hours, with a fueling stop in Japan.

Finally, with his boots on the ground, he was assigned to his platoon. They were introduced to the Montagnard Vietnamese villagers who helped and trained them in their specific jobs. He found the intense heat to be challenging every day. His job was keeping the runway operable. It was very difficult laying 1,000 feet of aluminum by hand. They would weld patches every night, repair and redo the runway for the aircraft to land the following day. Most pilots, including the commercial jet pilots, did not like landing on tons of aluminum matting. David's platoon faced incredible downpours of monsoon rains and scorching heat during the day. At all hours, they could see rockets launched. The base was built with walls around some of the perimeters, with a big hospital caring for the wounded from every branch.

Cam Ranh Bay had a natural harbor for the ships to port. Thus, all supplies and equipment were continually brought in as well as new troops. They would enjoy the beach during down time. Because of the porpoises there were no sharks. David remembers spending his first Christmas far away from home, with memories of his family being around the Christmas tree and the church sermons of Christ's birth. This was a very poignant time for him as he pondered his personal relationship; his Savior was closer to him than ever before. He still had a letter that was given to all the men in Vietnam from General, US Army Commander, W.C. Westmoreland.

The following is a copy:

COMMANDER'S MESSAGE

THROUGHOUT THE CHRISTIAN WORLD, THE CHRISTMAS SEASON IS A TIME OF JOY AND SPIRITUAL INSPIRATION. DESPITE SEPARATION FROM OUR

FAMILIES AND THE HARDSHIPS IMPOSED BY WAR, THOSE OF US IN VIETNAM WILL STILL SHARE THE TRADITIONAL CHRISTMAS SPIRIT THIS YEAR. WE CAN ENJOY THE SPIRITUAL SATISFACTION THAT COMES FROM GIVING. AS FIGHTING REPRESENTATIVES OF THE FREE WORLD, OUR GIFT IS THE HELP WE GIVE THE VIETNAMESE PEOPLE TO SECURE THEIR INDEPENDENCE, THEIR INDIVIDUAL SAFETY, AND THEIR FUTURE FREEDOM. EACH OF YOU GIVES A PART OF THIS GIFT AND DESERVES THE SATISFACTION OF HAVING INCREASED THE HAPPINESS OF OTHERS, THE TRUE CHRISTMAS SPIRIT. MY BEST WISHES TO EACH OF YOU AND YOUR FAMILIES FOR THE CHRISTMAS SEASON. MAY YOU ENJOY GOOD FORTUNE DURING THE COMING YEAR.

W.C. WESTMORELAND
GENERAL, U.S. ARMY, COMMANDING

David shared with me the craziness of the war, the battles that surrounded them, the wounded soldiers, and those that were shipped out in body bags. When he could, they would do humanitarian deeds, helping the villagers in need. He would often visit an orphanage that was run by the Catholic nuns. The nuns would walk the roads and pick up abandoned babies who were left by their mothers who became pregnant by American soldiers. David remembers how kind the nuns were doing incredible missionary work and always would have food to feed him and other soldiers who would visit their orphanage.

As far as the war goes, some memories just need to be forgotten. David remembers the famous weapons we had. One was called "Puff the Magic Dragon." It was a AC130, which had a Gatling gun that mowed down trees, the size of a football field. We also had a 40-millimeter shotgun that shot out armed "balls."

Control of the territory was the contributing factor of this war. Territory was lost and won every other day. We had to watch and suspect everything and everyone. The Viet Cong Military constructed bombs even in our compounds and built tunnels underground. The Agent Orange not only destroyed the vegetation but affected the soldiers and the people that lived in the surrounding rice paddies. The nights brought shelling that could rain fire over an area as big as a football field.

Returning to the states was a welcome relief, it was May 1968, and David said America never looked so good. No public "Welcome Home" party, but his family was thrilled that he was home safe and sound. David had saved his $50.00 a month salary and made a deposit on a new home. His memory of the war still carries heaviness and the few mementos fill a small briefcase, but he's thankful to be alive. He joined and helped in the support group at Los Angeles Air Force Station Tactical Air Command. After his service, he returned to his previous job as a firefighter.

David Stark, an honorable man who willingly laid down his life for his country and became a fireman after the war. He has since retired and wears his firefighter ring with pride. He shared about his illnesses due to being a firefighter, a condition from years of fighting fires, breathing the smoke and chemicals, which damaged his lungs and has affected his whole body.

Many military men and women died as heroes, as well as firefighters, but many more continue to live as unsung Heroes, lest we forget. We salute you Sergeant David Stark, not only for your brave service in the United States Air Force but also for your continued service to the firefighters of America. Your dedication to patriotism speaks loud and we are so very proud of you.

"But as for me, I watch in hope for the Lord,
I wait for God my Savior; my God will hear me."

Micah 7:7 NIV

JIM REALE
US ARMY 1966-67
CAM RANH BAY, VIETNAM

Patriotism doesn't end when war is over but is birthed and instilled in our inner most being. A patriot is one who supports their country and is prepared to defend it. Jim Reale is one such man. A football star athlete and Student Body President at Hawthorne High School, Jim was admired for all his achievements. One such achievement for Jim was marrying his high school sweetheart, a cute, vivacious cheerleader named Ruth.

When talking with him, you soon found yourself sitting in a comfortable, easy chair as he humbly describes his life. Aside from his athletic abilities, Jim had a passion for painting; it was a God given gift and a way for him to express his love for his country. His quiet, reserved personality continues to give accolades to others as he shares his story of the years in service and his survival tactics while in Vietnam.

Jim and Ruth had only been married six months; the date was January 18, 1966, a day they never forgot. They were celebrating Ruth's birthday when the mail brought an unwelcome draft notice. It was devastating news for them, and their joy changed to sorrow and sadness. The US was heavily involved in the Vietnam War—35,000 men were drafted into the Army that month alone, the largest draft in one month, Jim was one of them.

He was soon sent to Fort Mead, Maryland to endure his six weeks of boot camp. Being a great football player, he accepted the challenges and learned all the defensive modes to survive. In late December 1966, he boarded a ship from Oakland, California to Vietnam, a twenty-two-day voyage. He remembers the ocean was not kind, every wave and turn caused most of the men to be seasick.

This was no cruise ship; it was an old WW II ship, quite an experience. Space was confining and with every ocean wave, came seasickness beyond belief. Even while standing in line for the mess hall, men were constantly throwing up, which caused you to lose your appetite. He said of the 22 days at sea, he was sick 21 of those days, an unforgettable journey. The sight of land looked good as they headed to port at Cam Ranh Bay. Even though the imminent danger was ever so present, getting off that ship was such a relief, after all, he was in the Army, not the Navy.

He was assigned to transportation, and spent his year driving and transporting supplies and the troops of the 101st Airborne Division. They were also known as the Screaming Eagles, the historic light infantry division trained for air assault operations. He drove and traveled from Cam Ranh Bay to Da Nang and to Saigon and back. Being a driver was not his choice, but the Army saw fit for him to find ways to get the supplies or troops from one base to another. He estimates driving over 17,000 miles during his tour and counted his blessings every day he spent traveling making it from one point to the other, safely.

One drive took him and troops to a village on the border of Cambodia and Vietnam. As soon as they arrived, they were confined to the inside area and not allowed to leave. He describes these surroundings almost like a resort area, but outside the perimeter were the ravages of war with all its death and violence. It was like being in the eye of a tornado, where there seems to be stillness in the center but destruction beyond. Most soldiers took the motto of "attitude changes in Vietnam toward life." Survival modes surges, beyond anyone's imagination, he says, "you do what you had to do in war, and you forget what you did."

Safely returning to Cam Ranh Bay, he kept himself busy setting up camp with certain supplies. Getting their supplies and having the right equipment was imperative. One incident where they were in need of supplies, he approached his Captain to allow him to take a truck to commandeer supplies from Trang. He returned with a full load of supplies dodging bullets all the way.

His tour ended the following December 1967, and he was grateful his return trip was on a commercial jet. His bride, Ruth, gave birth to their first-born son while he was in Vietnam. Thankful that he survived, he looked forward to be with his newborn son and wife. In his later years, his passion for painting helped him to express his deep patriotic values, and love for America. His paintings describe what America stands for—life, liberty and the pursuit of happiness. His paintings sell at auctions and fund-raisers where he donates his proceeds to the Veterans Organizations. He and his wife will be celebrating 50 years of marriage. They have two sons and four grandchildren. He felt very fortunate and blessed to live the life he has lived.

Thank you, Jim, for your service, not only to your country but also to your fellow soldiers. You were a superstar in high school, and your humble personality speaks loudly of your character. What a wonderful legacy you have given to those who have known you. You have been blessed with a wonderful family and the ability from God to paint beautifully. I am so proud to have known you from high school. You were our hero then, and you still are our hero.

You may view or purchase Jim Reale's paintings at Jim-Reale.pixels.com.

"Finally, brothers, whatever is true, whatever is noble, whatever is right, whatever is pure, whatever is lovely, whatever is admirable-if anything is excellent or praiseworthy-think about such things."
Philippines 4:8 NIV

GEORGE REA
1ST LIEUTENANT US ARMY
VIETNAM DECEMBER 1968-DECEMBER 1969

A son, a husband, father, and soldier, George Rea was a gifted leader. As Class President of our 1962 Senior Class at Hawthorne High, he was admired and respected by his classmates and teachers. College was on his horizon, and during his 3rd year of college, he married the love of his life. Life was good, a happy marriage and baby on the way at the age of twenty-one. Military deferment was temporary; his draft status inevitably changed and in 1966 he was drafted into the US Army's Advanced Infantry. His intense training was at the Army base in Fort Polk, Louisiana also known as Tigerland. With a shaved head and Army's double-time "growl" march, he became proficient at shooting every kind of weapon. He was later afforded the opportunity to attend Officer Candidate School to become a First Lieutenant. In addition, George's leadership abilities led him to Ft. Bragg for five weeks to learn the basic Vietnamese language. Tragedy came while he was at Ft. Campbell Kentucky. Martin Luther King was assassinated in Memphis. The military was placed on high alert, and he was sent to Ft. Gordon to teach "riot control" to city officials in major cities.

GEORGE'S STORY

In December 1968, four days after our baby girl was born, I was deployed to Vietnam. Flooded with the emotions in leaving my family, I still can remember my flight over to Vietnam. My seatmate was another young draftee, and we watched the movie "The Odd Couple." We exchanged stories about our families and life back home. Laughter filled our heavy hearts as we watched that silly movie which helped in taking our minds off our destination. Unfortunately, I found out this young soldier was killed in action 3 days after we had arrived in Vietnam. I knew then that in the blink of an eye, my life could also be snuffed out. A reality check of what was ahead.

How do you describe a soldier's life in the jungles and rice paddies of Vietnam, a country that only knows war? Can you visualize or sense this incredible danger? The Viet Cong were a relentless enemy prepared to die for their cause. Life and death always hung in the balance. We faced death every day and never knew if this would be our last. The elements of the terrain were inexhaustible. The heat and humidity were suffocating. Traveling through the rice paddies, knee- deep in mud, filled with the infestation of mosquitos, big red ants, and venomous snakes.

Our c-rations were small but packed. Each contained one canned meat item, one canned fruit, bread, or a dessert, packet of cigarettes, matches, chewing gum, toilet paper, coffee, sugar, and a spoon. Not much substance and we were lucky if we got the fruit cocktail which was my favorite, supposedly each c-rations provided 1200 calories. It amazes me what memories stand out as we faced death daily. We knew that teamwork was critical and keeping our survival modes intact was imperative.

Although many of us men went to war with patriotic ideas, the reality of war became all consuming. The Army Republic Vietnam (ARVN) soldiers handled the war like a lifetime job. There were 400 Vietnam battalion army men, but like most jobs, only 350 showed up. Our job with our 350 American soldiers was Military Assistance and Command Vietnam (MACV). We would travel from village to village with the Republic Army. As the officer, along with a Sergeant and two American advisors, we provided general support and communications. The role of our team was to call in air strikes, medevac, and stay in touch with headquarters. As an interpreter among the Vietnamese army and villagers, I was obligated to eat out of politeness whatever was served to me during meetings. Eating their food was a big issue for me to conquer. Chicken soup was served with the chicken head and other parts floating on top. Their delicacy was "duck blood,"—as gross as it sounds—it tasted terrible and looked like brown Jell-O. At one very strategic meeting, I struggled to eat it, but my Sergeant leaned down and whispered, "Lieutenant, eat!" There were many occasions when I became very sick and vomited after eating their mystery meals. It was at those times when I desired a glass of cold milk to settle my stomach, and to this day, I cannot eat pig, eel, or fermented fish.

I vividly remember one of the most serious battles that my platoon encountered. We had received orders that a Viet Cong area needed to be searched. We began walking a 1,000-meter tree line forging our way through the jungles. While in a muddy, infested mosquito canal, we found ourselves surrounded by the Viet Cong. We began fighting an insurmountable battle, as the Viet Cong were above and around us. We called for helicopter back-up, and as we fought and waited, nightfall was upon us. There was an indescribable fear that the men and me were experiencing. Medivac could not get to us, and we had no choice, but to spend the night right where we were, drenching wet in the muddy waters. Words cannot describe this moment in time that could have taken all our lives. Surviving the night, none of us were wounded or taken prisoners, unlike the many pilots who were captured and kept as POW's.

Marijuana was prolific in the fields, not only did the Vietnamese use it, but our soldiers did too as a coping mechanism. Many of us have had our battles, drugs, drinking, sex, or incidents that happen because of war. However, smoking marijuana or use of heroin was and still is a punishable offense in all military branches.

On a lighter moment, I did my best to be a morale booster both out in the fields and while in camp. When things were quiet in the base, I would put up a sheet and show John Wayne movies. It was a temporary reprieve.

Rest and Recuperation (R&R) was a welcome five day relief, which took place four months after I had been in Vietnam. Part of my Lieutenant duties was to transport items from a fallen soldier to Hawaii. On this planned trip, I made arrangements to see my wife and baby. Seeing my wife and newborn baby brought me so much joy and peace. Hawaii gave me a feeling of being close to home, a place I longed to be. I held a deep desire to be with all my family. Saying my goodbyes to my wife and baby girl was incredibly difficult. I had to return to duty and finish my tour. I remained another eight months and could have taken another (R&R) but with only a month remaining opted to stay, returning home safely in December 1969.

I was able to escape the lingering effects of the war and completed my education at Cal State Long Beach, amid war protesters who were always on campus demonstrating.

The emotions and the scars of this war have never left me. There are situations that still affect me, but my family has been my best supporters. Being familiar with the Asian culture and as a language speaker, allowed me a long successful career with Toshiba, a Japanese company. Retired and enjoying the pleasures of life, friends, and family, are most important to me.

Thank you, George Rea, for always setting your standards high. Your abilities to learn languages were vital to the Vietnam War. Your sacrifices were valuable; you gave your all and your best not only in Vietnam but you leave a legacy for your family and friends. Thank you, and God Bless you.

"I waited patiently for the Lord; he turned to me and heard my cry. He lifted me out of the slimy pit, out of the mud and mire; he set my feet on a rock and gave me a firm place to stand."

Psalms 40: 1-2 NIV

BOOT CAMP BUDDIES

PAUL ROBINSON
1ST LIEUTENANT US ARMY
VIETNAM DEC. 68-SEPT. 69

As told by Lieutenant Robinson ...

A Midwestern guy, I was born in Michigan, but at the age of 21 headed to California in hopes of avoiding the draft for the impending war. I enrolled at San Diego State completing my first year and had been married six months when the postal service found me.

I entered boot camp at Ft. Polk, Louisiana. Bonding with other military guys helped us to survive. It was there

I met my buddy George Rea who talked me into going to OCS, Officers Candidate School at Ft. Benning, Georgia. We both agreed to sign up in hopes the war would be over after we finished. To our dismay, it was not, and I entered Infantry Training as a Platoon Officer. I was sent to Ft. Campbell, Kentucky where my specialty was mechanized equipment. I rode on the equipment as an armored personnel person.

Flying over to Vietnam caused much anxiety and natural fears, but my faith was strong, and it would be my faith that would be tested in the trenches of the jungles. I was assigned to a platoon who had just lost their 3rd Lieutenant in less than three weeks. They were quite indifferent to me and not at all interested in getting to know me, assuming I would be gone all too soon. Here is where I took a stand and told them that we would take care of each other— no drugs, and no alcohol, just watch one another's back. That's exactly what we did as the battlefields lay before us.

The very first month we engaged with a large group of the NVA's (North Vietnamese Army) between Saigon and the Northern part of Hwy 1. I had some in-country training before this battle and most of the Viet Cong were decimated after 1968's TET battles. Obviously, there were still many who remained as our next battle was in Ben Cui. As each of my men succumbed to wounds, they were transported to the closest hospital. As they recuperated from their injuries they returned to our unit, others whose injuries kept them from returning were sent back home. We did watch each other's back. Together we saved many lives, and our unit received Silvers Stars for their heroic actions. I was proud of my men and kept my word.

Chu Chi was another battle area I experienced. Most areas where our battles took place are tourist places now, especially where tourist can go down into the tunnels that were built by the North Viet Cong. We nicknamed the road into Chu Chi after Ann Margaret; who toured with the Bob Hope USO tour and traveled on these roads. We all knew where the Ann Margaret road was located.

Our unit earned another Silver Star during a large-scale encounter with the enemy. Our platoon had to pull back to allow air support to come in. Someone had noticed a soldier lying in the middle of the targeted area, and without hesitation, I headed back with my radioman running next to me. Finding the soldier, we dragged him to a safe zone. To this day, I never knew anything about him or even if he survived. I only know soldier's motto, "never leave anyone behind."

The photo of me in the picture of the APC (armored personnel carrier) was after we had just hit a mine. The spongy thing hanging over the side is what's left of the seat upon which I was riding. I was blown off, burned, and injured my back. There were two more mines on the very spot I landed, but God's angels held their hands over them while the medics were attending me. There can be no other explanation for not blowing up. After I was safely removed from the spot, they exploded.

Fear was always my dominant emotion. It gripped me from the beginning and remained until the end of my tour; I was reminded of a verse in Psalms 23, "Even thou I walk through the valley of the shadow of death, I will fear no evil for you are with me." I prayed daily for safety. I thanked God that we made it through another day and I asked for his protection during the night.

When any of my men got shot, I felt guilty and responsible for letting my team down because I promised I would take care of them. I lost two men in my platoon. It happened on a day I was not with them, and one was my driver. Emotions run deep! I could not shake the thought that if I had been with them, maybe things would have been different. A burden I still carry today.

My tour came to an end, and there was no difficult transition for me. The transition back to the state was on a C141 plane. Due to my officer status, I had to pay for my meals on board. It was Labor Day weekend, and I was processed quickly but failed the hearing test. They were going to detain me for several days, but I lied and said, my dad is a doctor, and he can work on me. I just wanted to get home. They released me, and I was able to catch a flight back home. After landing and picking up my duffle bag in the baggage area, a girl asked me, "Did you kill my brother?" She began yelling, screaming, making a scene and kept accusing me of killing her brother, the guy with her had to grab her and hold her off. That was my Welcome Home!

Despite that outburst, I was anxious to see my lovely bride who wrote me letters every day. Those letters were filled with her love and encouragement that pulled me through each day. I did not take the time to eat during my tour in Nam, and frankly, I often didn't want to eat. So, as a result, I came home 112 pounds lighter!

I returned to college, only this time to find demonstrators all over the campus protesting the war. I separated as a 1st Lieutenant and did not retire as I entered the Army Reserve, however after Vietnam, I found the Reserve quite boring.

My wife and I after 47 years of marriage have three wonderful children and five grandchildren. We have moved back to Michigan due to her health issues. My friendship with George has continued over the years. I also have been involved with reunions of those in my platoon. Every soldier in my platoon had been wounded and received along with the Silver Star, the Purple Heart. I am a man who is thankful and blessed with no desire to go back to Vietnam.

Thank you, Paul Robinson, honor and blessings to you sir, for your heroism and service. —BJ

"Now faith is the assurance of things hoped for,
the conviction of things not seen."

Hebrews 11:1

LARRY CUNNINGHAM, MARINE
GARDENA HIGH SCHOOL
GARDENA, CALIFORNIA

Larry Cunningham was my husband's classmate and wrote my husband the following excerpt:

I went to VietNam on a Continental Flight out of El Toro Marine Air Base, Camp Pendleton, California to Vietnam. I served in the Marine Corps from 1966 through 1969 and was in Vietnam in 1967-68. I was wounded in combat once, served as a squad leader, was awarded two Bronze Star's with combat "V" and Navy Commendation with combat "V." I saw a lot of combat as I was with the combat battalion 2/4, Second Battalion, 4th Marines. We spent most of our time up on and in the DMZ in what was called I Corps, top of South Vietnam. Was a long time ago and feel lucky that I came home but it's always with me and you never forget, believe me.

I do a bit of remodeling for friends, and one of the cabinet shops that I use has an owner that used to be a pilot on the Continental jet's that flew us over. It's a small world.

Thank you, Larry, for your service, may God continue to heal those memories. God Bless you! —BJ

"Peace I leave with you; my peace I give you.
I do not give to you as the world gives.
Do not let your hearts be troubled and do not be afraid."
John 14:27

GARDENA HIGH SCHOOL
GARDEN, CALIFORNIA
CLASS OF 1965

On the Vietnam Memorial Wall ...

KENNETH FRANCIS YBARRA, US ARMY
B TRP, 1ST SQD, 11 ARM CAV RGT
15 MARCH 1947 - 07 NOVEMBER 1968

LEONARD JAMES SUGIMOTO, US ARMY
WARRANT OFFICER
A CO, 25TH AVN BN, 25TH INF DIV, USARV
26 JANUARY 1947 - 16 DECEMBER 1969

MICHAEL F. GRAMLICK, US MARINE CORPS
LANCE CORPORAL
HMM-364, MAG-16, 1ST MAW
11 JUNE 1947 - 27 JULY 1969

Chapter 9

THE NEIGHBOR

PAUL, A VETERAN, AND NEIGHBOR
U.S. AIR FORCE 1964-71 VIETNAM 1967-68

A new home and new neighbors brought pleasant surprises. A tall, lean man slowly walking his petite dog up and down the street attracted my attention. Friendly greetings evolved into introductions and conversations that revealed his service in Vietnam. You never know what is behind a man's veneer. A face that was etched with his past, but a zest for life and a sense of humor that filled every sentence. The ravages of time have carried some physical difficulties, but with his witty humor and personality, one does not notice his slower pace.

As I sat with Paul to interview him, his wife, Shelly, sat by his side. This was her first time to hear details about Vietnam. As he began to share, her endearing touches and assurance were evidence of their special bond and love for one another. Paul's brother had introduced Shelly to him and after two years they were married in September, 1996. She listened intently as he humbly told his story.

"Where do I start?" was his initial comment. I began the questions: "Tell me a little about yourself?"

He proceeded to share that he was raised in Buffalo, New York and told me a little about his father who had served in the military during WWII. After Paul graduated from high school, his father encouraged him to enlist in the Air Force. He was off to boot camp at Lackland Air Force Base in San Antonio, Texas where he spent six weeks in his introduction into military life. He laughingly tells us the Air Force was the right choice for him when the "obstacle course" was postponed due to cold weather!

After boot camp, he made a short visit back home to regroup with family and affirm with friends his decision to join the military. "I was a tall young man, but now in my uniform, I seemed taller, he laughingly recalls." I returned to Shepard Air Force Base for training in classified communication as a "crypto technician." This specialized training was for teletype equipment repair that led him into his career with the Air Force and later with commercial airlines. He learned and specialized in repairing and restoring sophisticated Air Force communication equipment. The Air Force relocated him to the cold land of Alaska far from the shores of Vietnam. As the war progressed, scary as it was, he felt compelled to volunteer. He says he was no hero. He was just doing what was right, feeling patriotisms and duty calling. After additional combat training, he remembers his flight from Oakland, California Air Force Base to Saigon. It was on one of the commercial MAC flights and easily could have been on a Continental airplane. The long flight over gave him time to reflect and feelings of apprehension, knowing the dangers ahead. He recalled looking out the window on final approach into Saigon and seeing massive ground artillery and he knew they weren't playing games down below.

After landing and going through his orders, the Air Force asked, "Why are you here?" They continued to tell him this was not his assigned base and sent him to Pleiku Air Base. He was then placed on a military flight, which was a short hop in-country to Pleiku. Jokingly Paul says there were no stewardesses on that flight! After his second arrival, he was again asked, "Why are you here, your assignment base is DaNang." So for the third time, he was transported via the roads to the central highland region of DaNang. Escorted in a vehicle traveling on a dry, barren road, filled with hidden dangers left that were from the Viet

Cong, he continued to say he was definitely in the warzone and was immediately told, "See anything suspicious on the passes, shoot it, but use judgment."

Trying to find his final destination was not a leisurely scenic drive, but a harrowing experience. Traveling the roads and seeing the jungles gave him an eye level view of the ravages of this war. He was glad his weapon was by his side. Realizing the imminent danger that now surrounded him, it was an indescribable feeling when his boots hit the ground in DaNang. His orders and papers finally accepted, he settled into his barracks. Peaceful days and nights were now a thing of the past, constant bombings and battles were all around him.

He began working on all the sophisticated equipment. Paul humbly describes his job, as "no big deal." In all actuality, his job was very important as he equipped the men in the fields and on base with the technology that was needed for that time in history. Paul was in his element and gradually became accustomed to his surroundings. The weather he said, "was hotter than hell, along with the unending rain that lasted for days."

Every day brought new challenges, besides the war, bartering and trading were a normal occurrence on base. Everything was negotiable, from cases of steaks to teletype equipment. Entertainment was far, and few, and the troops looked forward to the possibility of Bob Hope's USO tour. The guys would get together to drink and make the best of their evenings at the NCO Club. Paul added, with "blood, sweat, and cheers." When the bombings got too close, the club and golf courses were closed. I stopped writing and asked, "Golf course?" "Yea," Paul continued to say, "that never went over well with all the guys." Paul's eyes twinkled as he says, with a wink, "Only in our dreams, there was no golf course."

Paul goes on to describe the location on base was well equipped and somewhat safe for a war that had been raging for thirteen years. It was January 1968 and the South Vietnamese troops, and allies looked forward to a traditional seven-day ceasefire for their holiday that was called Tet. It was a Vietnamese celebration of their New Year. The morning of this holiday, the North Vietnamese troops and Viet Cong forces made an all out attack on cities and towns in South Vietnam. This was the biggest assault since the beginning of the war. Every city and every base received a barrage of severe rocket and mortar attacks. This attack made it difficult for us to work on the sophisticated equipment. There were no safe barracks or facilities; it was a very fearful and stressful time. We were issued M16 rifles and clips of ammo to protect ourselves and secure our perimeters.

Courage is doing what you need to do in fear. Paul took his time and with all honesty shared that he had never been so scared and even shook with fear. The mortars and bombs kept coming every ten to fifteen minutes. We were on the defense mode, wearing our bulletproof vest flack jackets, sleeping with our ammo and boots on. Because of all the bombings with the vibrations on the ground, it was not possible to work on the electrical equipment. We left and went off base to an abandoned bunker in Tent City, an old French facility. We were able to do the precision work without the ground shaking, returning to home base only to shower and shave. How long did this continue, I asked? "Seemed indefinite, days upon days." He continued with, "Hell of a lot of rockets came in ..." then paused, as if he was looking back, reflecting on moments that he purposely forgot.

After reflecting on surviving that episode, he then changed the topic and began sharing the days he took for R&R. He told us about traveling in-country to Monkey

Mountain that overlooked the Bay of DaNang near China Beach. It was a beautiful sight that brought him momentary peace, something he had not had since arriving in Vietnam. In the midst of peaceful scenery, surrounded by the elements of war, he had to return fire at the enemy who was hidden in the bushes..

His tour ended in Vietnam in 1968, but reenlisted in 1971, however, he was diagnosed with diabetes and released from duty to TDL (temporary duty retirement list). Returning to the states in 1973, he continued to work on equipment and remembered his transition to civilian life took time. He made the adjustment with the help of his humor, knowing that laughter lightens heaviness.

His innate abilities led him to a life-long career with major airlines. Retiring from the airlines, "time" did not stand still for Paul. He opened and operated a clock shop, continuing to repair and restore, old antique clocks. As we finished the interview, Paul made one last statement, "I have a desire to return to Vietnam, but due to my physical limitations, it's not possible. "

Through the American Legion Post 379, and annual reunions, Paul has formed friendships with other Vietnam Vets; they have a bond that ties them together.

God Bless you, Paul, thank you for your years of service. Your country honors you, and we honor you. We call you our hero! God has another way of saying this:

"Come to me, all you who are weary and burdened and I will give you rest."
Matthew 11:28

Class of May, 1968, BJ front row center

Early years of flying—affluent apartment

Meals hand-carried

Having fun between flights

ONE POW's 2,030 DAYS OF SOLITARY IN CHINA

VIETNAM

ARMY NURSE
CAUGHT IN THE
LINE OF FIRE

TET
The frontline fury
was everywhere

A Huey's wild
duel with a VC
.50-cal gunner

'Don't shoot—
it's A Company!'

Surrounded by
NVA (and rats)
at Camp Carroll

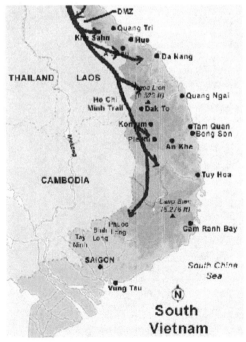

South
Vietnam

Map of Vietnam

Chatting with soldiers parked near aircraft

BJ ready to board troops

Linda George, BJ, & Marsha Stemler in Vietnam

BJ & Sandi Kramer

Continental Flight Attendants, Russie Mitchell and Sheri Carlson

MAC Aircraft Boeing 707

Okinawa

MAC Boeing 707 on runway in Philippines
Photo courtesy of Steven Grimes

Captain Tom Schuchat, US Air Force Pilot
Penny on Graduation Day

Tom & Penny Schuchat

Paul Galanti
LIFE magazine editors airbrushed out both fingers
for fear of repercussions.

Paul & Phyllis Galanti

Colonel Tony Wood
USMC Retired

Congressman Sam Johnson,
Colonel USAF, former POW

BJ meeting Lieutenant General Richard Carey, USMC

Paul Robinson

Paul Robison's APC hit by mine

Hawthorne High Football stars

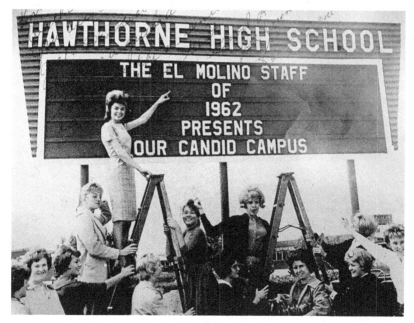

BJ on ladder

Sergeant Dan Dye, US Army

Sergeant David Stark, US Air Force

David Stark LAFD

Paul Brown, US Army, "Bad start, new ending"

Jim Reale, US Army

Heroes from High School - David, George, & Dan

Uncle Mike (Sunny)
Granillo, Germany
WWII

BJ's cousin Johnny, killed in
action Vietnam, 1967

BJ's cousin Mike Granillo

BJ's cousin, Michael and Albert Granillo,
served in Iraq and Afghanistan

BJ with Michael Langan and Beagle Bailey in Hawaii

Captain Bill Otter, US Army & wife, Jo, in Hawaii

American Legion Post, Home of the Brave

Paul Rabe (USAF) and his wife Shelly is "the neighbor"

Sharon Singstock, Miss Wisconsin, 1965

USO Tour

Sharon and her brother Dave with the USO Tour

Sharon entertaining the troops

USS Gallup

Commander David Singstock, US Navy

David Singstock in Saudi Arabia

BJ & her brother, Bob Elliott

BJ & her brother at Cam Ranh Bay, Vietnam

Chapter 10

THE MEN FROM
THE AMERICAN LEGION POST 379

Paul Rabe, our neighbor, introduced me to the Vietnam Veterans at the American Legion Post 379 located in Bedford, Texas. I had the honor and privilege to meet the following veterans who shared a part of their stories while in Vietnam. I was very impressed with their support for one another and their bond of friendship.

Mike Garlington	Brian McCormick
Mike Regan	Robert Bowles

MIKE GARLINGTON
US ARMY SPEC4
VIETNAM 1968-69

On my second visit to American Legion Post 379, I found myself passing the wall of history with the names honoring those who served and died. Glancing to my left, the bar stools were full, and the familiar smell of tobacco and beer filled the air. Walking back to their large ballroom, my eyes adjusting from the dark entrance to the well-lit room, I located a table to meet and interview another vet. While arranging my notes and recorder, a jovial, happy guy strolls in with a drink in hand. He introduced himself as he sat down directly in front of me. He had a broad smile on his face, his eyes were bright, and it was obvious that he wanted to share his Vietnam story. His friendship with the other vets was evident when one by one they came in and sat at the table with him. These other vets were not privy to know each other while in Vietnam, but through the years here at the Post, they have built a friendship. With my questions and tape recorder lying on the table, it was easy for them to observe the interview with Mike Garlington, US Army Spec 4, Vietnam 1968-69. As told in Mike's own words ...

I am an Arkansas guy, born 1943 in Little Rock, Arkansas and grew up in El Dorado. As a teenager, I fell in love with music and my guitar. This led me to form a local band at a very young age. After graduating from El Dorado High School, our band was fortunate to be booked at the Peppermint Lounge, in New York City. It was a popular discotheque on 45th and Broadway that brought in many celebrities who would drink and dance the night away. It was the launchpad for the famous global twist craze in the 60s. I remember one night when John Wayne himself with his Texas swag, came in—the same night as Liza Minnelli. John Wayne bought each table a bottle of whiskey and later that evening, I danced with Liza Minnelli and Diana Dors. Our gig lasted eight weeks and held a lifetime of memories for me and the other guys in the band.

Returning home from New York City, I entered the University of Arkansas and played my guitar in many dorms on campus. We had a college classmate who loved our band music so much she flew us on a private jet to Japan to perform at her wedding. The language difference did not seem to be a barrier as we played and partied. Music is truly the universal language.

I graduated with a Masters Degree in English and taught school the same year when I met my wife and moved to Texas. The Vietnam War was going on, and even though I was able to avoid the draft for a time, inevitably I was drafted February of 1968. Boot camp was at Ft. Bliss, Texas and there was no time to even think about playing my guitar. The perks of being a college graduate enabled two of us from our unit to continue further training at Hunter Army Airfield base in Savannah, Georgia. Anxiously aware that Vietnam was our next destination, orders came for deployment. I left on a commercial MAC flight out of Ft. Lewis, Washington that flew us to Japan then into Cam Ranh Bay.

Upon my arrival, it was discovered that there were no orders or paperwork for me. I immediately volunteered to return to the states but to no avail and two days later I was sent to Chu Lai. The unknown fear factor gripped me; the sounds of bombings, seeing wounded soldiers and smelling gunpowder that drifted in the air around me. My thoughts every day began to consume me with the anticipation of being wounded myself or killed.

My assignment was initially working in carpentry, refurbishing the Commander's hooch, his living quarters. I was able to get a guitar and began playing in my barracks. One night my Command Sergeant came in and heard me playing. That evening changed the direction of my military career. I still had guard duty but was now performing and playing my guitar regularly on base.

The perimeter of this base was located at the edge of a mountain that went straight down into the ocean. Guard duty meant we had to gear up with our M16 weapons and hang on the cliffs during the night. The Viet Cong would use small round boats with approximately three to eight VC's per boat. They would paddle to the bottom of the cliff and proceed to climb the mountain where we would knock them off any way we could. The adrenaline in me was so high that I could hear the pounding of my heart. I was under extreme duress. The threat intensified during the pitch dark wondering if I would be shot while hanging down this 150-foot cliff. We shot flares to light up the ocean below, allowing us to see the enemy and return fire. In the daylight, we would pull the bodies from the water and destroy their small boats. This fighting went on night after night taking a toll on all of us.

Playing my guitar back in my barracks helped release and calm the fears that we faced every night. Music is the language of the soul, soothing not only to myself but my fellow soldiers as well.

I was able to take a couple of R&R's, once back to Hawaii to see my wife and once to Hong Kong. In Hong Kong, I stayed at the Humphrey, a 30-story hotel. I went to have a drink in the bar where a local band was playing, of course, I asked if I could sit in and ended up playing the whole week with them. I was back in my element, the war was distant to me, and I was enjoying this time immensely. There were other interludes for downtime to help us cope with the intensity of the war. The Huey Gun Ship helicopters took us to larger ships outside the perimeter of our base allowing soldiers to decompress. We turned in our weapons as we boarded a ship and got drunk for three days. We were completely safe from rocket attacks, felt secure and finally able to sleep.

During one three-day reprieve, a "slick" helicopter landed with a band and equipment to entertain the guys. Dragging off guitars and amps to set up, I immediately walked over and asked if I could sit in. After performing with them for an hour and a half, they suggested that I ask my commander back at base to try out for the Command Military Touring Trio Band. When I returned, I was granted permission and flew to Saigon for the audition. Accepted as their guitar player, I became part of this touring band. My new role in Vietnam had been drastically changed from soldier to performing full time for the troops. Our music was used to comfort and entertain. We traveled to multiple bases and hospitals, wherever the troops were, we played.

We were transported by aircraft carriers to various ships including the Kitty Hawk and Enterprise. Our band performed in places where no other USO Tour was allowed to go, due to the seriousness and extent of wounded soldiers. At the hospitals, I would play until the early hours of the mornings. One particular hospital, where we had performed for hours, the other guys finally left to get some sleep, but I just kept playing. Never had I seen such hunger for a touch of the outside world. The "burn ship" victims impressed me the most as I witnessed incredible sufferings of these men burned beyond recognition. The human spirit amazed me that they could survive the injuries that were beyond description. I could see in their eyes their horrific pain and suffering.

Mike took a moment in the interview at this point as he began to choke up, recalling the smiles on the wounded men's faces. This was an incredibly touching and emotional moment for him. These performances gave him a clear vision of his mission and purpose—it was for these men! His trio band did a total of 144 shows in Vietnam. He also performed on three radio stations and a couple of TV spots.

My transition back to the states was somewhat difficult; I saw so much in Vietnam. My life was never quite the same. There was no Welcome Home banner, no parade, absolutely nothing, I put everything away and didn't talk much about Vietnam. I cherish every day now and don't allow pettiness or little things to bother me. I went to work for Zale's Corporation in October '69 as Director of Marketing. I created and produced mail programs for two years. During that time, I met and connected with a sales representative who referred me to Dun and Bradstreet in California. I worked for them for 15 years. It was during this time that I was hired to be a technical advisor in Hollywood for Kurt Russell who starred in the movie, Elvis. I taught him the chords, techniques of playing and holding the guitar, a cool experience for me.

My wife and I had two children, however, we divorced after 20 years, due to my character flaws. Moving back to Dallas Texas, I am retired now and still enjoying playing my guitar for local events and at the Post 379.

I would like to go back someday and visit Saigon, Pleiku, and DaNang. The true beauty of the land without the ravages of war would indeed be a sight to see. Vietnam Vets see life from a different perspective, we lived in a difficult wartime, in an unsettlingly and hostile America.

IN MEMORY OF
CHARLES MICHAEL GARLINGTON
12/17/1943-6/23/2015

Each Vietnam Vet deserves the Medal of Honor and Recognition. After the interview, I gave my thanks to Mike, for serving our country in Vietnam. I thanked him for using his talents and giving the gift of music to so many soldiers. You were brave on those Mountain Cliffs but even braver while performing for the burned victims. Where words fail, music quiets the heart and washes away the dust of the day.

In Loving Remembrance, Mike Garlington, 71 went to be with our Lord, June 23, 2015. Mike loved his country and served honorably in the U.S. Army from February 1968 to October 1969. He was a singer as well as a guitar and harmonica player for the bands, The Jokers, TC & The Slicks, and Mike & The Misfits from 1950s through 2015. Mike was an active member of the American Legion Post 379 and served as Adjutant for two terms. He married his soul mate, Gail DeCarli on June 22, 1990. They shared 25 wonderful years together. Mike was a gentleman who loved people and lived his life, his way, embracing every moment. His family and friends truly miss him. The last song at his memorial service was by Louis Armstrong, "What a Wonderful World." It brought tears to everyone's eyes.

"Greater love has no one than this, that he lay down his life for his friends."

John 15:13

BRIAN MCCORMICK
US ARMY 9TH INFANTRY
VIETNAM 1966-69

My name is Brian (MAC) McCormick, US Army, 9th Infantry E 5 Specialist (Buck Sargent) I fought many battles in Vietnam and continue to fight personal physical battles today. I grew up a Syracuse New York kid who was the oldest boy of nine brothers and sisters. My mother in my eyes was a saint, attending Catholic Mass daily. We were the typical large family, everyone with their assigned chores depending upon age. Growing up in upstate New York where the streets were our playgrounds, playmates were our siblings or neighborhood kids. Our evenings were spent in the kitchen where mom was cooking or helping us with homework. My mom and dad's hard work kept our family together. Life began to change for our mother at forty when she was diagnosed with multiple sclerosis. She struggled with this illness for ten years dying at the young age of 50. There was no easy way for us kids especially the younger ones to handle this enormous catastrophe. Shock, grief and complete sadness engulfed us all. I was working for an accounting firm and had to quit my job to return home and help my dad with my younger brothers. I went to work for the local telephone company. Anger and bitterness towards God overwhelmed me, even though I don't attend church today, I still believe in God.

It was May 1966, a year after my mom's death, when I received my draft notice. After giving notice to work, within weeks, I was sent to Fort Dix for boot camp, ready with my tough experiences, to fight the world. At Fort Riley, Kansas I was trained to prepare a unit for the battles to come in the Mekong Delta. It was here; we boarded a Troop Train that took us on a three-day cross-country ride to Oakland, California. The train rolled right up along side the USS William Weigel, a WWII troop transport ship. Security was tight, as we filed on board, securing our belongings in the hold of the ship. It was not very comforting to know that we were about to cross the ocean in a ship that was built in the 40s. The Weigel had seen a lot of sea action, so I trusted it to be seaworthy.

Leaving San Francisco Bay, cruising past Alcatraz prison then under the Golden Gate Bridge seasickness overtook us. The top bunk, among the six bunks, saved me from the projectile vomiting. Once out to sea, we had hoped the adjustment to the ship's movement would not affect us as much. Coke and saltines were the most popular menu item on this twenty-two days journey. Crossing the International Date Line brought new challenges and experiences. The Navy troops said we had to graduate from a tadpole to a frog, so we had to go through an initiation ceremony, quite humiliating, less said here is best. It took eighteen days to travel to Okinawa where we were allowed to take a short shore leave to get our "land legs" back. After eight hours it was back on the ship, we had to get our "sea legs" back while contending with our "alcohol legs." It was three more days to Vietnam, where we became the first ground troops in the Mekong Delta.

Our 9th Division Infantry developed Camp Bear Cat base, home for many military units located near Bien Hoa. Adjusting to the 125-degree weather was not easy. Pup tents were home until we could build larger sandbag walls around the tents. As the first unit in the delta, our mission "Operation Enterprise" was to secure four or five areas. So, the engineers would come in and have us build a base camp, about one per month; then we would move to the next site. The first few months were very scary. I rarely slept, jumped at any sight or sound never knowing if this was my last day. We lived out of our Tracks, an armored vehicle or our pup tents. There was no mess hall, bar or theater and I lost weight eating only c-rations. My specific job for nine months was APC (Armed Personnel Carrier) doing search & rescue and secret patrols in the Mekong Delta. I became a mortar observer for three months only because of the degree of danger. The radio was a must for my job as well as carrying all my weapons. There were constant explosions around me. Soldiers incurred injuries from the enemy and also from friendly fire. One friend was killed in a bunker next to me. A platoon consisted of 150 soldiers and over 50% would lose their lives. Out of my unit, 17 were killed. Our Division fought in the worse conditions securing and developing airfields, new bases, as well as building our own bunkers. I was then transferred to the FDC (Fire Direction Control) where I plotted the directions for our guns. For every one man in the fight, nine others were doing the logistics. I served three months out of Bear Cat in the jungles around Saigon. We would attempt to locate, engage and destroy the enemy along with their supply lines. This was difficult to do because the enemy tried to avoid major battles where he was "out-gunned" They preferred to set booby traps, snipe at us or ambush small patrols where he had us outnumbered. When we were under heavy fire, we called in the Air Force, the Huey Gun Ship or Cobra Gun Ships that had machine guns and rockets. Part of every Search and Destroy mission was the Medical Evacuation helicopters called "dust-off" for the wounded or dead soldiers.

Some missions were on Eagle flights. We would go from one helicopter to another spending nights in bamboo fields. One night, I heard a bang, the radio operator found a grenade wrapped with bamboo, everyone said don't do anything, but he moved, and the explosion killed him instantly. He was only three feet from me. After three months, you start getting this attitude of, "I don't give a shit" that last until your close countdowns, less than 60 days. There were many causalities, and it was dangerous to be around short-timers with less than a month remaining. Search and Destroy Missions were an everyday job.

Sleepless nights in the deep dark jungle were the original "fright" nights, Overwhelming fear of what crept near you kept my adrenaline at a constant high point. A reprieve was my R & R. I flew to Malaysia where entertainment was always available, no further details needed.

My last assignment found me back in the jungles near Saigon; I knew my days were short, and so did my fellow soldiers. Word came to return to base and board the flight back home. Still cautious making my way back to base, I call this moment in time (cross over) carrying my duffle bag and weapon, my fatigues were almost reddish yellow from the dust, Agent Orange, and dirt. I remember filing by the new recruits in their new dark green jungle fatigues and not being able to look them in the eyes. We ambled along; all of us darkened by a year of intense sun and aged by a year of hard combat. There was no way they could perceive what they were going to encounter. "God help them!" I thought.

It was shortly after Thanksgiving, 1967 I returned home somehow changed from this war. Fortunately, I was able to return to my same job with the Telephone Company and remained 37 years with Verizon, retiring in 2001. The first ten years after Vietnam were very difficult; I was plagued with anxiety and PTSD (Post Traumatic Syndrome Disorder). Lung disease wears on my body possibly contracted from Agent Orange. I married my love, Joan, in 1973 and we have two wonderful children.

Returning to the local American Legion Post, I am able to find mutual camaraderie with other Vets. The annual reunions find lots of tears and serve as great therapy for each man. Asked if I would ever return to Vietnam, absolutely not, that battle is over.

Brian, I thank you for your service and sacrifices you made during Vietnam and the many years that you continue to fight health battles. God loves you, and so do the American people. —BJ

"For God so loved the world that he gave his one and only Son, that whoever believes in him shall not perish but have eternal life."

John 3:16

MIKE REGAN
AIR FORCE E4 BUCK SERGEANT
VIETNAM 1966-67

Choices can either make or break a man. As a youth, I was a troublemaker and a handful for my dear single mother. In my teen years, I attended an all-boys Catholic school but was asked to leave at sixteen because of my behavior. The public high school made no difference, as fistfights became a routine. I eventually quit school, but my choices were limited, jail or military! Too young to enlist, my mother signed for me, a blessing in disguise. At seventeen, I joined the US Air Force, passing the entrance exam with high marks, it was 1963, and my path was set. Security and explosive detection were the fields I chose at Lackland Air Force Base in San Antonio, Texas. Under the DOD (Department of Defense) and Security Police School, over a period of three years, I learned to train dogs for Vietnam. Our unit became known as the Night Fighters (the dog handlers). In 1966, I volunteered for Tan Son Nhut, Vietnam, a three-month test with the dogs. We flew forty-two dogs over on two B52 bombers. It took days to make this flight, landing, refueling and situating the dogs at each stopover. After arriving in Vietnam, we immediately went into training, getting the dogs accustomed to the scents and sounds of the jungles, calling this mission, "pigs and people." Our training included every aspect that men and dogs would encounter. We had special tunnel dogs, underwater dogs, and jungle dogs. During this three-month training, no dogs were lost. With the success of this mission, I began to travel back and forth to Thailand, (Vietnam West) training new dogs. We continued to customize the training for their assigned task. We started receiving dogs that were trained for police and sentry duties. The sentry dogs were trained to hate everything, trained to attack and kill on command. The only way to get the dog off someone was to choke it.

Ho Chi Minh Trail was especially dangerous. Our dogs could distinguish the scent of our urine versus the Viet Cong and alert us. Everything was very dangerous for us; the jungles of Vietnam were horrific and scary, especially at night. During the rainy season, we lived in wet fatigues that would dry when it stopped raining. During the day, our fatigues would be covered with orange spray from Agent Orange. It was miserable being by yourself with only your dog. I had a lot of conversations with God, especially in my "fox holes." My dog was posted around me at nightfall because the Viet Cong would try to sneak in to kill us both. I would ask God to give me strength every night to maintain and survive. In pitch darkness, my dog would direct me to an enemy's position where I would fire my M16. Sleep deprivation was ongoing, and it was vital to follow your dog's instincts—it meant life or death. To choose your instinct over the dogs was suicidal. My dog and I fought a lot of tunnel battles together, sometimes alongside the Army. I would use an M1911/45 weapon in the tunnels, and the dog would come out dazed because of the deafening sounds of the shots.

The only way I stayed alive going back and forth from the Air Force bunkers to the jungles, was because of the alertness of the dog. During the battles, I would communicate with other soldiers via radio clicks. Silence was key to avoid ambushes. I also used the M18 Claymore, a small ground weapon that would detonate a bomb dispersing lethal steel ball bearings up to a distance of 100 yards. It would kill or maim enemy ground troops. However, my preference was hand grenades that had a kill- zone of up to 16.5 feet.

The value of the dogs was demonstrated daily. There were times when my dog and I escorted doctors or nurses to area perimeters. The dogs could smell danger, and we had to trust their abilities to keep us safe. My dog was always on patrol, smelling danger that became my ticket out alive. Each week after returning to the bunkers, my down time was sharing events and stories of the week with the other "night fighters." Sleep was never easy or long even back at base, then there were the Malaria tablets, that invariably would give the GI runs.

As the tour of each dog handler soldier ended, it would take me thirty days to retrain another dog handler. The sentry dogs out of Thailand would bite anything or anyone and were the most dangerous. The new soldiers had to be trained to handle these dogs by muzzling them and to get dominance without getting attacked or killed themselves. I remember when it was my final day to hand over my dog to his new handler. For both their survivals, toughness had to be swallowed by me without showing any emotions. Spending months and nights in foxholes, living in the jungles, knowing your dog was always on patrol created an attachment. This difficult transition was part of the end process, and it was gut wrenching. Packed and ready to leave Vietnam on the plane we called, the Freedom Bird, I was still filled with anxiety and averted eye contact as I filed past the "newbies" coming into the war. I believe they could see the heaviness of the war and the toll it had taken on us. Yes, we had been through a lot, beaten down, yet thankful to be survivors. One of my good memories while in Vietnam was listening to a 'Mars' radio announcer, 'Fast Eddie', and years later I was able to reunite with him in Germany.

Returning home was quite an adjustment. Recovering from living in the jungles was not easy. I remember going to a mall and experiencing my first anxiety attack. I was somehow able to calm myself down and soon learned that I had PTSD (post traumatic stress disorder). Physically I have difficulty in breathing, due to the Agent Orange that I inhaled while living in the jungles. Our fatigues were covered in the orange dust. I also have been diagnosed with prostate cancer and continue that battle today.

When I returned from Vietnam, unfortunately my marriage ended with a friendly divorce; we had one son. The stress from the war was too much for me to maintain my marriage. I met and married Eileen, who helped me get through emotional and mental trauma of the war with her love, prayers and encouragement. I love you Eileen! We had two daughters and I am blessed with grandchildren. I worked for the Police Force for 30 years, as Chief Master Sergeant and retired in 1993 as a coordinator. I still have PTSD attacks, but with help and over time, it has become less and less. I am living the best life I can, enjoying my family and friends. The Legion Post 379 allows me camaraderie with those men that fought the battles for the freedom we now enjoy. I support, 'Old Dogs and Pups' with the Vietnam Security Police Association.

Thank you, Mike Regan, for your service and sacrifices in Vietnam and serving our country for nearly 30 years. Your service to the Police Force was also appreciated. God Bless you. These Bible verses spoke loudly while writing your story, taken from the NIV Bible:

"Keep me as the apple of your eye;
hide me in the shadow of your wings,
from the wicked who assail me,
from my mortal enemies who surround me."
Psalm 17:8

"Even though I walk through the valley of the shadow
of death, I will fear no evil, for you are with me;
your rod and your staff, they comfort me. You prepare
a table before me in the presence of my enemies. You
anoint my head with oil; my cup overflows. Surely
goodness and love will follow me all the days of my life,
and I will dwell in the house of the Lord forever.
Psalm 23:4-6

ROBERT BOWLES
US MARINE
VIETNAM 1966-67

Born and raised in Texas, I am a homegrown guy, who enlisted in the Marines four days after graduating from high school. The year was 1966, and Camp Pendleton became home for nine weeks of basic training. Normally, boot camp was thirteen weeks, but we were at war, and everything was a rush. Exiting, boot camp as a Lance Corporal, I was trained as a rifleman and rocket launcher. Feeling proud and honored to be a Marine, I returned home to Texas for farewells parties with my school friends and family. Orders for deployment to Vietnam gave me feelings of trepidation of what lay ahead. It was December 1, 1966, when our unit boarded a Continental Airline's MAC flight out of Travis Air Force Base in California. With discipline and politeness instilled in us, we filed orderly and politely on board. We were trained Marines.

Flying into DaNang and landing at night in the pouring rain was my introduction to Vietnam. We had to be processed and were told to find a bench to sleep on for the night. The morning light broke the darkness, and I realized a goat had found a comfortable place to sleep next to me. Most of my time was spent in Hoi An, a village south of DaNang. I was assigned to the 1st Battalion, 1st Division where I did 19 operations. I was the assault man, and rocket flare thrower, blowing up the Viet Cong in their tunnels. The Air Force taught us the use of the M16; an assault rifle developed for use in the jungle. Overcoming the emotions of fear mixed with bravado, I quickly had to learn to survive the jungle, heat, humidity, and countless insects. Frustrations over lack of enough ammo and constant fears were magnified with soldier's depression at Christmas.

Our state of mind was always at risk; each soldier reacts differently to war. My feelings fluctuated between highs and lows. On September 27th, our unit was sent to the DMZ the dividing line between the South and North Vietnam that was supposed to be a combat free area. The military term DMZ (Demilitarized Zone) in all actuality was where we encountered many battles and losses.

My scariest and most challenging mission was October 1967, "Operation Medina." We were embarking on a search and destroy operation near Hai Lang forest, filled with deep valleys and hills. Surrounding us at night were the bug infested jungles and all it's heavy humidity. However, the beauty of this area would have been an awesome sight had it not been for the war. This day's activity was at an all-time high, and we grunts (military term for infantry) knew something big was about to happen. We started this mission after two days of climbing up and down hills. Nighttime brought us to a very fast moving river. The only way across was to hang on to a rope strung across the river. I was carrying 85 pounds of gear in this dark murky water that got deeper and deeper sucking my boots with each step. Holding my rifle over my head with one hand and only able to see three feet in front of me, I was gripped with fear. As Marines, we made this tedious trek "Semper Fi" (always faithful) and staying alive became a priority. The night lasted forever, and it was always spooky beyond our perimeter. I was fortunate to make it across without getting shot, wounded or attacked. Foxholes with a canvas top became my bed for the first 90 days. Lizards became my friends because they ate mosquitoes and I realized how thankful I was for those malaria shots. "Operation Medina" marked the beginning for many, including myself of a life filled with pain and sadness. Multiple engagements with the enemy occurred.

One of the biggest fears was getting caught in the countless booby traps used by the Viet Cong. Missing family and home cooking were another one of the voids felt by many of us. If lucky, we would have a hot meal every two weeks, ham and Lima beans. On other occasions, we became proficient at heating some food on the engines of our trucks. After "Operation Medina," my last engagement took us back to the DMZ. The engagement there brought a sense of impending danger. I dug the deepest foxhole in the hill. At sundown, a B52 flew overhead notifying us of imminent danger of a large Viet Cong army heading our way. All hell broke out! We left our foxholes to draw the enemy out while the B52's dropped bombs on them. The devastation was all around us; there were bodies, bombings, smoke, and dirt everywhere. The Viet Cong blew up our landing field so our first job the next morning was to clear and repair the field. We did it just in time for a light bomber aircraft to land. We quickly boarded it and flew to DaNang.

My tour ended on Christmas Eve 1967 when I returned to Travis Air Force base. I remained in the military for eight more months, and this helped me in the transition to adjust from the warzone. I served a total of three years 1966 to 1969 and was able to get out 85 days early because of my time in Vietnam. Receiving a Campaign Star for actions in Vietnam, I was thankful to have made it home. It took years before I could eat ham and Lima beans again.

Once back to civilian life, I began working for the telephone company. The little things don't bother us anymore, what is important is family, friends, and fellow vets. You never forget the war or the men that fought the battles with you. I am retired and live life as best as I can. Pray there will never be another Vietnam War.

Robert Bowles was born February 1948 in Dallas, Texas and grew up in Irving. He graduated from Coppell

High School.

Thank you, from all your Vietnam Veterans at Post 379. America thanks you and I thank you for your remarkable, brave service. You are honored and respected; God Bless you. —BJ

*"The Lord has been my defense and my God,
the rock of my refuge."*

Psalms 94:22

Robert Bowles passed May 19, 2017 to Post Everlasting. He was actively involved in Post 379 and was loved by all.

Chapter 11

HAWAII & DIVINE APPOINTMENTS

The chilly days of January in Texas brought thoughts of a sandy beach and warm weather. Hawaii was a spontaneous choice. My 40-year career allowed me flying privileges and within 48 hours I was on the beach of Waikiki. A few days to relax and write my Vietnam stories were my plan. While unpacking, I soon learned that I had brought the wrong stories and thought to myself, "oh well, I'll sit at the beach and read a good book." God had other plans—divine appointments that brought about amazing encounters in meeting other Vietnam Vets.

In the early hours of the first morning, I stepped onto the balcony looking directly up to huge white clouds that were speeding by overhead as though on a secret mission. They were an incredible sight. I was awestruck and began to pray, "How mighty are you God, thank you for bringing me here. I have no agenda Lord, this is your day, let me do your will." I began to sing praises to Him like never before. At sun up, I readied myself for a stroll on Waikiki beach to a favorite breakfast place of mine, the Shorebird. I had acquired a Vietnam Vet hat last year and proudly wore it. I couldn't help but remember so many years ago, on these same beaches, spending my time partying and sunbathing while the Vietnam War raged on! How blessed I felt today, my life filled, returning to Hawaii with a desire to write about those that served and those I may have served aboard the military MAC flights. Even though the sands of time had passed, I felt such an enormous peace and freedom as I walked barefoot on the sands of Waikiki wearing my Vietnam hat. Every Vietnam soldier I encounter brings me pride, thankfulness, and restoration. The following pages illustrate these remarkable encounters.

DOG TAGS AND DOG TALES: HAWAII JANUARY 15, 2015

MICHAEL LANGAN

A beagle is a beagle, but this one was very special. Beagle Bailey was his name. He was an emotional help dog I soon learned. While strolling through the lobby of a Waikiki hotel, my eye caught this happy little dog. Everyone including kids surrounded him. I too went over to this sweet Beagle dog, with his wagging tail that invited love and affection. Bending down to pet him, my eyes were drawn up to the man holding his leash. He seemed pleased by all the attention given his dog. A tall, tanned man with a handlebar mustache and blondish ponytail met my eyes as I saw his Vietnam Vet cap. His piercing blue eyes and inviting smile drew me into a conversation. I asked, "When were you in Vietnam?" He responded, '69 to '71. I explained that I was a stewardess transporting the troops to Vietnam with Continental Airlines those same years. He said he remembered flying on "Continental Airlines" and to this day remembers the smell of the sweet perfume the stewardess was wearing throughout the flight. I laughed not knowing how important that smell would be to him later in life. As he began to tell me of his flight, I thought, this Vet could have been on one of my flights. I started praying, my heart pounding, as I shared with him about writing my book. Standing there for a few moments in silence, I asked him if he had time to talk? He briefly thought about my question and then said, "Yes, I have time. "

Beagle Bailey in tow, we found a quiet corner to hear his story and what a story I heard. Unprepared without my tablet, I quickly rushed to the front desk where they freely gave me large blank pieces of paper. Meeting Vietnam Vets never seemed awkward, but rather comfortable for me. There is a bond I feel and can't describe. I always want to know where they were stationed, which branch they were in, and what their duties were. I have come to realize that every job of a military soldier is vital to the advancement of our freedom.

As we walked through the lobby to sit down, his quiet demeanor portrayed his deep thoughts and reflections of what he was about to share. "I've only talked to one other person about Vietnam and that's my psychiatrist," he said. My heart knew he had seen many battles and was still in combat within himself. We found a quiet place to sit inside the bar area that was not opened. I have been touched by many stories shared by Vietnam Vets but his story tugged at my heart and emotions even more. I pray that justification and closure are possible to the many unknown vets of this generation as each story is told.

Not having my routine questions with me, I just went with the flow...some of the questions that I have asked didn't seem important right now as he began telling me about those years that still haunt him.

Michael Douglas Langan is my name, I was in the Army, and served in Vietnam for two tours. My father was a 30-year veteran of the Army, as a Command Sergeant Major, ROTC instructor (Reserve Officer Training Corps). The youngest of three boys, we traveled worldwide because of my father's career. As a young boy, I remember living on bases in France, Germany, and Japan. It was hard on my mom, uprooting and moving us three boys. I found it difficult to make lasting friendships. The authority and discipline my father lived by in the military, unfortunately, carried over into our family life. The strictness and rules of our home pushed us to leave as soon as we could. After my graduation from West Side High School in Omaha Nebraska, I followed suit with my brothers and dad by enlisting in the Army.

After boot camp, the Army flew me over to Vietnam on Continental Airlines. I was eighteen years old and the stewardesses were pretty cute and young. The sweetness of the stewardesses brought some consolation to where we were going. The levity of the crew, the good food, the sights, and smells left an indelible impression on me. Each time I fell off to sleep, I would wake smelling perfume worn by the stewardesses as they passed through the cabin or when serving our meals. It took three flights to get us to Vietnam and each flight brought about new stewardesses and more food. I still remember each flight had brownies and a carton of cold milk.

After arriving in Cam Ranh Bay, I was assigned to work in supplies, this made me feel better knowing I would not be fighting in the jungles. My assignment had me confined working in a small trailer and I soon found out that I was very claustrophobic. I was reassigned to a medical supply truck, taking supplies and drugs to wounded soldiers. Living on a base surrounded by the terrain of this new country took some adjustment. Meeting the new guy next to my bunk I realized the importance of the buddy system. We learned how imperative it was to watch each other's backs because the jungle was not our friend. Carrying three different weapons, an M16, a 45 in my shoulder holster, and a 38 special on my hip I headed my emergency resupply truck into the fields of battles. The classifications I held allowed me to travel by any means possible, ground or air, to reach the wounded with supplies. There was only one person who could outrank me and that was the President of the United States. At times we fought our way through the gates of hell to reach areas of wounded soldiers. Wounds included those who had been bitten by animals. If possible, we would cut the animals head off to be checked for rabies, unfortunately, most animals carried rabies and the guys had to endure six weeks of the very painful injections.

I was under extreme pressure aiding the severely injured soldiers in the midst of battlefields. Bullets flying overhead, gunfire, and bombs going off, vibrating our ears and head. We were always driving in haste while defending our medical supplies. Young intruders along the road would jump from motorcycles onto our trucks stealing what they could grab with knife in hand. We met their advances with our weapons, securing our cargo and delivering the supplies was utmost critical for our men.

As Mike continued to share his story, he stopped and paused as he said,

"The most traumatic incident for me was when I was in Saigon at the 3rd Field Hospital."

Mike related ... I was ushered into the bedsides to give morphine to the soldiers who were hit by the napalm bombings. Our soldiers would get caught in the napalm bombs and receive the most devastating burns that mercifully took their lives in many cases. Napalm bombs are a jellied mixture of aluminum soap powder and oil or gasoline used as an incendiary in bombs. When the bomb would hit you, the acid explosion would disintegrate your uniform and then continue to burn your skin down to your bones and then some. It was the worse kind of suffering and it took a lot of morphine, more than what we had, to subdue the agony of pain. The hospital room echoed with their cries for help and I felt brokenness hearing the agony in their voices. I began by telling them they were going to be all right, over and over, but after awhile I stopped saying it. Administering the morphine didn't stop their pain. I felt helpless and to this day these horrific scenes replay over in my mind as I wondered if we did enough to save their lives and their sufferings.

As I continued to write Mike's story, I soon was caught up with the things he started to tell me regarding his bunkmates.

He continued ... I had three and one by one they each were killed. Losing each bunkmate was like losing a part of myself. It started to become very difficult with each new replacement. I would ask myself, "When would be my last day?" This was a very difficult time, losing buddies and daily fighting our way to deliver medical supplies. The battle I faced every day was not just physical but emotional as well. Depression overtook me as I now had lost three friends to this war. One afternoon while sitting in my hooch, (thatched hut) by myself, feelings of despair overwhelmed me. Thoughts to end my life were so strong that I picked up my weapon and placed the barrel to my head. I was ready to pull the trigger when a new recruit walked in. This wide-eye young soldier dropped his duffel bag and said, "I am your new recruit." I said, "The hell you are and shot him in his arm." I was not willing to lose another buddy, so who saved who at this moment in time. My life was spared not only from killing myself but spared from going to the brig for my actions. I was given my own hooch and volunteered for the hot LZ (Landing Zone) where the likelihood that you would be shot was 100%. I didn't care anymore; my motivation was to get the supplies to the wounded any way possible. I worked alone, as the only supply soldier, doing mission after mission. Traveling to the LZ by helicopter only, the loudness of propellers was deafening. Daily challenges left me numb and crazy. I would wake up each morning saying, "How many lives can I save or is this the day I die?"

My commitment to serve with the medical unit in Vietnam extended for two tours. My transition to stateside was very difficult. Being immersed in the war, then coming back to normal civilization was not an easy adjustment. Feeling all alone, I did not want my mom to see me. I withdrew from society, became paranoid, kind of lost myself, and did not want to communicate with anyone. My health deteriorated. I had nosebleeds every night and woke up each day with a ring of dry blood around my mouth. I soon found out that I had received concussions from all the air strikes, bombs, and the noise from the helicopters. The concussions caused pressures in my eyes and bleeding from my nose and mouth. All my senses were adversely affected. Besides my hearing loss, the lack of taste and smell had permanently gone which created a challenge to determine fresh foods in my refrigerator. I continue treatments and meds at two VA hospitals twice a week for PTSD.

The lasting effects of the war brought the need for my support dog; Beagle Bailey. His sensitivity training allowed him to comfort me during my times of anxiety. When Bailey climbs up on my lap with licks and love he helps me to cope each day.

I live my life nowadays walking my best buddy on the beaches of Waikiki. I meet people, talk and try to enjoy each day as best as I can. Even though the scars of the war are embedded, I have learned to live with my injuries and disabilities. I have few regrets, but truly know that I helped hundreds, if not a thousand of wounded fellow soldiers. Hooah!

Thank you, Mike Douglas Langan, for your sacrifices and thank you on behalf of every soldier you helped in Vietnam. In the midst of battles, you and others continued to deliver the most precious treasure, the medical supplies that saved lives. Who would have known that your childhood upbringing would give you the courage, strength, and fortitude to endure this incredible mission? Your father and mother would have been very proud of what an awesome soldier you became. You have a Hero's HEART! I pray healing and restoration over you. May you be able to smell flowers, food, and fresh cut grass once again in Jesus name. God Bless you! —BJ

*"Those whose hope is in the Lord will have renewed
strength; they will grow wings like eagles;
they will run and not grow tired."*

Isaiah 40:31

DIVINE APPOINTMENT NUMBER TWO

CAPTAIN BILL OTTER
US ARMY

Being the first in line is a must to secure a beachfront table at Chucks Steak House on Waikiki. This has been a long time favorite restaurant, eating on the Veranda with the ocean view, palm trees and watching the sunset. Did I say great food and Hawaiian music! It was there that I met a charming couple with the same goal. As the doors swung open, they smiled and pointed to me to go first.

While dining, I realized the best photo of Diamond Head was over this couple's corner table where a short friendly conversation ensued. After finishing their meal, they stopped to talk a minute. This cute couple was endearing and friendly. My thoughts were still on my earlier Vet interview; I asked him if he had been in Vietnam? Curious as to why I asked, I explained, seeing your hat, thought it might be military? His feisty spirit and response surprised me, as he leaned down with a smile on his face and said, "Yes, I was in Vietnam."

I shared about my book and asked if I could interview him? He said yes, and because they were leaving the next day, suggested that we get together that night. We decided to meet poolside in thirty minutes. How incredible was this opportunity, what were the chances, the odds of standing in line and meeting a fellow Vietnam vet, I called this divine appointment number two.

Paying my check, I quickly went to my room to retrieve my tablet and was at the poolside of the Outrigger to write his story.

Every night is gorgeous in Hawaii; the moon was bright and the evening air was wonderful. We gathered around the pool, his wife, Jo with a glass of wine and book in hand, settled in her lounge chair. He had methodically lined up chairs and towels—military organization at its best. I thought this would be a short interview but hours later; I had listened to stories of a Lieutenant who took his duties seriously in unprecedented conditions.

My curiosity always began with some basic questions to find out about each soldier. This is the story of Captain William (Bill) Otter, US Army, who served in Vietnam 1966-67.

I was raised with two younger sisters in Deerfield Illinois, a suburb of Chicago. My dad was an Officer in World War II. Following my father's lead, after graduating from Loyola Academy in Illinois, I pursued a college that offered a ROTC program (Reserve Officer Training Corps) I chose John Carroll University in Cleveland, Ohio where I attended four years of the ROTC program. In the summer between my junior and senior year, I enlisted in the US Army and was sent to Fort Indiantown Gap, Pennsylvania in 1964 for my initial boot camp. After boot camp, I was able to return to college and complete my education. It was there I met my sweetheart and my future wife. I graduated with a BS (Bachelor of Science) and BA (Business Administration) and was commissioned as a 2nd Lieutenant in May 1965.

We found out that nearly all the Officers in my class were going to Vietnam. It was a new war, and there was much to be learned. My active duty began with a ten-week course, where I was sent to Fort Eustis, Virginia; home base of Army Transportation Corps, for TOBC (Transportation Officers Basic Course). My next assignment was to Granite City Army Depot as Assistant Transportation Officer. Granite City was a support base for the Red Ball Express, 72 hour delivery of critical items shipped from the US to Vietnam. I then became a platoon leader at Fort Lee, Virginia, where we mobilized a new company, the 47th Transportation Company-Medium Truck-Petroleum. One of the jobs of a platoon leader was to train incoming soldiers to drive the 5,000-gallon fuel trucks. Most of these eighteen-year-olds had just learned to drive a car before they went to basic training and AIT (Advanced Individual Training). Some did not even have a driver's license, and we were training them to drive 5,000-gallon fuel trucks. We were mixed grays of officers and non-commissioned officers and were part of what was termed "The Build-up" (the large rapid movement of military units from the USA to Vietnam).

We received orders to ship out the trucks and equipment to Hampton Roads Army Terminal in Virginia. The tanker trucks and our unit equipment were placed on ships that sailed from the Atlantic Ocean to Vietnam. Several days later, we left out of Richmond Virginia on a chartered MAC flight to Oakland, California. There, we were transported to a ship where I vividly remember sailing under the awesome Golden Gate Bridge. However, it was at this point where many of the 7,000 men aboard, including me, became seasick. Even though the USS Edwin Kirkpatrick was a fast ship, I believe, the voyage was an arduous seventeen-day journey. Crossing the International Dateline was a cause for a crazy rite of initiation and celebration with my shipmates.

When we arrived in Vietnam, the weather was stormy, and the seas were rough. Our ship swung at anchor for two days in heavy rainfall. We were told this was Vung

Tao. We finally boarded landing crafts with all our gear and were taken close to shore. The waves were rough and the monsoon rains did not help our visibility. We had to jump off the ramps of the landing craft into the water that measured up to six feet, carrying everything over our heads, our duffle bag, rifle, and ammunition. The sun was setting quickly as the black stormy night engulfed us. In what seemed to be an impossibility, 7,000 of us made it safely to shore. The sounds of the crashing waves and pounding rain, camouflaged any sounds we made. Reaching the beach, we were exhausted and quickly dropped our gear. We had no idea where we were, other than we were somewhere near Vung Tao. All unit organization was lost, we had no orders or communication, we were mixed up and scattered. Wet and cold, we ended up securing ourselves hidden in bushes, off the beach and spending the night on alert. During the night, we faintly heard voices in the distance, believing they were probably Viet Cong. When the sun came up, transport planes were roaring overhead; we discovered to our amazement and embarrassment that we were on the perimeter of an improvised US military landing strip. Those voices that we heard through the night were US soldiers and our unit became the brunt of jokes.

In spite of this confused arrival, we waited through-out the day until C-119 transport planes arrived and flew us north to Bien Hoa Air Base. There we boarded two and a half ton trucks, (deuce and a half's) as they were known and were transported to a base camp at nearby Long Binh where we quickly set up our barracks. Long Binh was the major logistics and supply base for III Corps area. It was expanding quickly during the "Build-up." Our organizational skills and training kicked in, and plans were quickly put into action to get the 47th ready. Two other companies like ours (the 556th and the 538th) had been in camp for some time and were struggling to meet the rapidly increasing daily demand for fuel. All three of these companies combined were now responsible for transporting fuel to the military units in III and IV Corps area, which was the whole southern half of Vietnam.

The arrival of the ship with our 60 tanker trucks along with the other vehicles equipment, allowed us to go into full operation. Being methodical, every afternoon when orders were received, the operations staff of each of the three companies (556th, 538th, and 47th) would assign the tractors, loaded fuel trailer, drivers, and assistant drivers to various destinations for the next day's missions. Most trucks would be assigned to join one or more convoys to specific destinations. Other trucks would be used in local service between Saigon and Bien Hoa Air Base and operated individually in the civilian traffic.

The job of delivering fuel to the front-line units was vital. We prided ourselves in meeting our daily commitments. We knew lives depended on getting fuel. Each soldier's job was imperative and pertinent to our mission, no one less and no one more; we worked as a team. A company consisted of about 200 soldiers and although we had only been together for a few months, I began to know each man by name. Every soldier was important, doing their jobs was critical to our mission. We worked hard, ate on the run and delivered the fuel to the front-line units' base camps. In the dry season, we ate a lot of dust from the dried laterite (a red clay material) road surface each day. On rainy days, it was slippery red mud. Delivery of each load of fuel made the day a success.

There was also the job of tending to the trucks that had broken down along the way, taking them in tow with a spare tractor, unloading them at the destination and getting them back to base for repairs. We always tried to return from the convoys, pass through downtown Saigon and reload the trucks at the large Shell, Esso, and Caltex fuel depots at Nhà Bè, south of Saigon. We then drove the loaded trucks back to our base camp at Long Binh for maintenance and an early departure the next morning. Most of the time, the commitments for the next day's deliveries were received at our base camp several hours before we returned from the day's mission. The high demand for fuel required us to keep the trucks fueled each night. Maintenance and repairs were also performed after we returned to base. Besides repairs, we changed flat tires (usually 3-8 flats per night per truck company). Driver's responsibilities and shop maintenance were a top priority every night.

Our maintenance standards were high. Of our 60 fuel tankers, we had to have 57 or 58 available every day. The other two or three would be held back for scheduled maintenance or repairs. All our vehicles had to be kept in excellent running condition. No one wanted to be broken-down in "Charlie Country." Blowing the sand and dust out of the air filters, changing flat tires and replacing damaged or failed parts was an on-going routine. Our fleet maintenance was better than the conditions in the Supply & Transport (S&T) companies; they were the flatbeds that hauled the ammunition weapons and supplies. We sometimes had to pitch in and help those units deliver their cargo when they couldn't get enough trucks running. The routine was to get the vehicles loaded, bed down and move out before dawn on the next day's convoys and missions.

Mid-way through the year I was "in country," I was transferred to the 556th to replace a lieutenant who had left. The 556th was the oldest unit that had seen a lot of service with old, worn out trucks. The 538th and the 47th both pitched in to carry the load until the new trucks with new officers and men arrived. We delivered fuel to Long Binh, Bien Hoa, Cu Chi, Tay Ninh and several other base camps. Tay Ninh was very close to the Cambodian border. We also ventured out on other special missions in support of the front-line units.

Silently with a pause from his orderly verbal remembrance of his Vietnam days, Bill's voice became subdued as he told me about an incident that he regrets, responsibility and guilt that he still carries. "War is not fair and with it comes consequences and mishaps; he begins to tell me about the incident." Bill continues, this particular day's activities were bustling; the weather was hot and humid. I had been out with a large group of 556th trucks on convoy all day as had the other two platoon leaders. When we pulled back into base camp in the evening, I went to the operations tent as I was also the company's Operations Officer, checking on our next day's operations. The Operations Sergeant informed me that one of our convoys had been attacked and we had casualties. My heart sank with the news of this occurrence, up to this point we had operated without causality to any of our men. Many thoughts were rushing through my head, who, how and where did this happen? My heart was pounding as he explained to me, that these were two eighteen-year-old soldiers. He told me their names, which I did not recognize. I asked if there had been a mistake? No, Sir, no mistake.

These two men had arrived in our base after all the convoys had left that morning. They were replacements, and I had not met either one of them. I was informed they had not been briefed or trained in our procedures. An emergency order for fuel had been sent to us early that morning after the convoys had all left. These two new men and four of our regulars were assigned to drive two fuel tanker trucks and a Jeep being led by one of our sergeants. Once the small convoy arrived at its destination at an airstrip base along Highway 13 in the Iron Triangle, it was diverted directly out into a forward base camp area in what we were told had been the Michelin rubber plantation. The jungle canopy was very high and our normal mission at that time was to deliver only to base camps. The units in the camp bases would distribute the fuel in smaller quantities to their forward outposts.

While navigating the muddy jungle trail with the heavily loaded tankers, the first truck hit a land mine which exploded, blowing the front axle and wheels off the tractor. Both new men were badly injured, and the combat unit evacuated them in "med-evac" choppers to an unknown location. The second fuel truck was also damaged, and the convoy was unable to proceed. The vehicles were left along the road, and the men were evacuated out to the airstrip. The news of this tragedy hit us all hard. We had been in country for nearly a year without any manpower losses in our unit. This felt like a blow to our armor. We were a tight group, following strict regulations. We transported jet fuel (JP-4), high-octane aviation gasoline, diesel fuel (DF-2) and regular gasoline ("mogas"). Violations meant causalities. Heavy-hearted, the next day, another sergeant and I, plus six men drove two tractors without trailers, and a wrecker to recover our losses. We joined a larger convoy for the trip to the airstrip. There we reported to the officer in charge and told him our mission. He informed us that the area was not secure and that it would take his forces a few more days to clear the area. On our third day, we followed the guide-jeep out along the muddy road into the plantation. We found our vehicles, but none of our men. The four that were not injured were delivered back to our base camp after we had left. We worked at the site loading the wrecked tractors, transported them the next three miles or so to the forward base camp and unloaded the fuel. We returned to a point where our guide told us to wait, he would take us back to the airstrip, but our guide had not returned by nightfall. The eight of us huddled and decided we needed to stay quiet and dark. That meant, no lights and no chatter. We knew we were sitting ducks, unsecured, and at risk.

During the night, a mortar and artillery battle flared up in the trees near us. A friendly forward outpost that we could see through the trees was firing on an enemy's position, and they were attacked by Viet Cong with mortars. Afterward, the outpost was quiet and the shelling and mortars stopped. We stayed dark and silent and wide awake. At day break, a Major in a jeep arrived and told us to follow him. We slowly drove by the remains of the forward outpost; Charlie had taken its toll on those men. War is hell, sights, and smell of death lingered in the air.

The next day, finally arriving back at our base camp, I met with our men who had made it back to camp okay. They told us their story and rescue. They had no idea where the two new soldiers who were injured were taken. These men were the first and last causalities from our unit while I was their Platoon leader. Despite several inquiries over several weeks, I was never to learn the fate of these two young men. We did, however, have to deliver their personal gear back to the replacement center for forwarding. Not knowing what happened to them has always disturbed me. I still have remorse and guilt. After this incident, changes were made to procedures at headquarters. This was the first, and it was to be the last time that a middle-of-the-day unscheduled mission was placed on any of the three truck companies by the higher headquarters.

R&R was a time (5-6 days as I remember) for each soldier to leave Vietnam and go to a nearby country outside the war zone to relax. It was very necessary for mind, body, and spirit. It was a time to let defenses down and enjoy life outside the turmoil of the war. Bill shared, he went to Penang, an island off the west coast of Malaysia for his R&R. He said," it was a good feeling to download and be released from my duties." However, my few days of R&R slipped away all too quickly. The hot salt water and the sunny beach was healing to both body and soul. I had to remind myself of all the accomplishments that our unit had done in such a short time. All of us in the 47th, the 538th and the 556th derived satisfaction from knowing we were meeting our commitments to the front-line units each day. The realization that our fuel tankers were a vital part of this war was a good feeling and accomplishment.

About two months before the end of my tour, we were very busy and overall, at least in our base camp, things seemed to be running well until one evening about 1900 hours when a horrific battle scene erupted right in front of our fences along the base perimeter. We were fighting for our lives. It all started earlier that morning shortly after the female villagers arrived. They came daily to clean tents and wash laundry. They were trustworthy and loyal to us. That morning, they were all-downcast and could not look at us with their eyes. They appeared very frightened; one girl even had tears in her eyes. They were trying to go on with their work, but they were unusually silent. We started comparing notes with each other and decided that this could be some warning to us that something was very wrong. We were not sure, but we put the word out to be extra vigilant just in case. Unfortunately, we were correct. That evening we found out the hard way that the Viet Cong had invaded the nearby village and were holding family member's hostage.

The quiet night was shattered by a barrage of gunfire as machine guns, and rifle firing erupted. On the other side of the perimeter road along our camp fences, the mortars started landing nearby. Our neighboring unit lost all four members on a gun jeep patrol while on the perimeter road at our fences. The shots seemed to be coming from the nearby village. We returned short range fire and avoided firing into the village because of the friendly villagers, some of whom worked for us. We called for supporting pre-planned artillery fire to be dropped into the field between our camp perimeter road and the village which was lower than our camp site. Unfortunately, the first two friendly artillery rounds fell short damaging our perimeter fence and started a fire on one of the loaded tanker trucks in our motor pool parking area. Everyone in camp not defending responded to the motor pool. We were able to put the fire out and stopped the leakage.

Help came from "Puff the Magic Dragon" (Nickname for the C-47s that flew slowly above without lights) as they began dropping parachute flares to turn night into day. Then the cannon fire from Puff began with tracer rounds mixed in among the others tracing a dashed red line to the ground. Puff pounded relentlessly. Then the adjusted artillery fire began pounding the field and the village. After about three hours, all got very quiet. We watched and waited, expecting a second attack. We reinforced our rear perimeter forces and our east flank, figuring Charlie might try to surprise us from behind or the side. In the morning, we began inspecting our defenses, our camp facilities, our trucks, repairing damage and cleaning up the motor pool. We had no information on enemy losses if any? We soon learned that the Viet Cong had extended their tunnel system from the river to the village. However, the field between us and the village and the area between the village and the river received daily "attention" from US aviators packing a punch. Charlie kept his head down after that night. In a few days, several of the girls and a few of the men returned from their village to resume work in our camp; some did not return.

My tour was ending here in Vietnam; I was looking forward to returning to the states because my college sweetheart and I had made plans before I left to marry when I returned. She took care of all the arrangements, and all they needed was me, the groom. I had not been told my exact departure day from Vietnam but knew it was near. When my orders came one afternoon in October 1967, my convoy was late returning to camp from refueling in Nhà Bè. I only had one and a half hours to pack up my gear, clear camp and get to the processing center at Bien Hoa Air Base. You did not have to tell me twice. I made a transfer of my duties, gathered my gear, bid my unit farewell and started moving to Bien Hoa.

I was allowed one phone call before leaving Vietnam. I called my mom to tell her I was coming home. Her voice sounded wonderful, and I had to pinch myself to realize this was happening now. I was leaving Vietnam 14 days before the date I had been expecting to be replaced. A sign of relief came over me as I boarded that commercial jet. It was a Continental Airlines Boeing 707 stretch of some sort and "The Proud Bird with the Golden Tail" never looked so good! When the gears went up, a spontaneous applause came from all of us. Homeward bound, safe and sound at last. Five hours later, we landed on Okinawa where we fueled up and changed crews and headed east over the Pacific.

We landed at Travis Air Force Base in California, northeast of the San Francisco Bay area. I didn't care that it was an Air Force base, we were all in this together. The mission now was to clear processing and be released from active duty. Once done, I joined others quickly boarding a chartered bus that took us directly to San Francisco International Airport. Quickly moving off the bus, there were four of us who were catching the flight to Chicago. Still wearing the uniform, we wore when we left Vietnam, we had less than fifteen minutes to catch an American Airlines flight that we were told was loaded and waiting at the gate for us. As we ran down the concourse, we encountered anti-war protestors, who spit in our faces with remarks that had hate in their voices. My fists were clenched, and I was ready to fight, but we all decided in a split second that getting home was more important than responding to those guys. There were no cowards in Vietnam; we had grown up a little and learned to pick our battles. We made the flight, and the cabin door closed behind us. After boarding the aircraft, we learned that the Captain had made an earlier announcement that he was taking a delay and explained to the passengers there were four soldiers who needed to board this flight. We got a good American welcome. We were home now! The flight attendants treated us with extra kindness, and it was good to finally be going home.

Homecoming with the family and my soon to be bride was a wonderful distraction from the war. Our wedding day was great, and upon returning from our honeymoon, I began my working career for Chicago & NorthWestern Railroad in Chicago. I loved railroads (still, do) and this was a giant step toward fulfilling my life-long ambitions in the business world.

A life-long railroad career, the love of great parents, a lovely wife and five wonderful children who have given us seven grandchildren (so far). Blessed to have met good friends along the way, all have been the best gifts a man could ever hope for. It has given me the incentive to try to practice the values that have made our Country great and strong. To remember all those who have served and given everything that we might enjoy freedom. Lest we never forget!

Author's note: Love has no beginning and no end. Bill and Jo Otter celebrate their lives, first from college, then the war in Vietnam, marriage, and blessings from their five children. Success and a career never eluded Bill as he still works in the business arena as a railroad consultant.

Thank you, Captain Bill Otter, for your dedications and service to your country and fellow men. It was an honor to meet you and your wife Jo in Hawaii. I was proud to write about your service and sacrifice in Vietnam. I realize more and more that each branch, each soldier is critical to the importance of our military. You served our soldiers and country well, as the Bible says, *"Well done, good and faithful servant."* Matthew 25:21

Thank you for being patient with me while writing your story with our many corrections. God Bless you! —BJ

Chapter 12

MY BROTHER AND I IN CAM RANH BAY

Cam Ranh Bay was one of the most serene places we landed in Vietnam. It is nestled in South China's deep blue sea, located in the middle of South Vietnam. The beauty of the landscapes and the beaches overshadowed evidence of war. The base and runways were totally built by our troops and maintained daily.

In the beginning, landing at Cam Ranh Bay seemed safe and uninterrupted by sounds or sights, unlike the other bases. However, the war became more personal after my sister informed me that our brother Bob had enlisted in the Army and was based in Cam Ranh Bay. I had mixed emotions wondering if I would be able to see him? My phone bill soared that month as I made calls to everyone who could make this reunion possible.

The call from scheduling came informing me that my next trip would take me into Cam Ranh Bay. I was overwhelmed with joy. I continued to contact the Army, informed my family and left on that trip with anxiety and anticipation. Being separated from my brother most of our childhood, memories and thoughts of growing up raced through my mind. Sibling love could finally reconnect in this distant country.

The flight over felt different to me and the crew knew my excitement of seeing my brother. The morning of our trip into Cam Ranh Bay was extra extraordinary for me. I awoke early, dressed quickly and waited anxiously for the transportation to our aircraft. Prior to our landing, our Captain made the call to operations, notifying our impending arrival and informed them that one of the stewardesses on the flight had a brother who needed to be contacted. Later I found out that as soon as my brother was notified, he quickly left his desk and came out to the airport waiting for the arrival of our airplane. After the troops deplaned, the other crew members took over the duties of cleaning the cabin and allowed me ten minutes on the tarmac. I hurriedly made my way down the steps and when I saw my brother, flew into his open arms. He looked handsome in his fatigues and had the biggest smile on his face. My brother is two years younger but looked so mature. This was an incredible moment, embracing one another with hugs in a country that was on the other side of the world. Who would have ever thought something like this could happen.

He informed me of his administration duties and assured me he would not be in combat or fighting in the jungles. I was relieved that he was not in the infantry. His year at college helped him with this position for the hospital on base. We were able to see one another several times and as long as there was a chance to see him, I continued to fly the MAC Operations. I had hoped for many more flights into Cam Ranh Bay, I even alerted scheduling back in the states to assign me trips into his base. Continental Airlines had a procedure of assigning trips to crew members similar to military procedures. It was called Fifo in and Fifo out, meaning first flight in would go to the bottom of the crew lists and you would not be assigned a trip until your name came up to the top.

On one of the trips, my brother's face showed some signs of bruising. He shared with me that they had an episode. While at his desk, a grenade was thrown into the office area blowing up the filing cabinets. He said he was not seriously injured and assured me he was OK with only scratches. Trying to wrap my head around this incident with only ten minutes on the ground was scary and overwhelming. Taking off on that flight was not a good day for me as I worried about how close this war was hitting home and my brother shared his concern for my safety. No one is safe in warzones.

All was well between my brother and me until the black market photo of me resurfaced in the barracks on his base. Remember those photos that I posed for in my Hollywood years, well they surfaced all the way over to Vietnam. My brother was devastated and contacted my sister. She called informing me that my brother was upset with these photos. It was an awkward and unsettling time for all of us. Unfortunately, my brother and I didn't see one another again in Vietnam. Our love for each other moved us beyond this incident, as war, life, and death took precedence. I kept those photos secret throughout my flying career and hoped they would never show up again.

To this day my brother rarely if ever, talks about Vietnam. Like so many Vets, those days are not things they want to remember. Only years later while he was undergoing major surgery did his "tough guy" emotions he learned in Vietnam surface. He is thankful to be alive and I could not be more proud of my brother and the years he served our country. He married a lovely lady and raised three wonderful children. He unselfishly gives back to his community as well as his commitment to the organization of AA. Bless you, Bob, I love you.

"A heart at Peace gives life to the body"
Proverbs 14:30

ROBERT A. ELLIOTT
US ARMY SPEC 5
SERVED TWO TOURS IN VIETNAM,
OCT. '68-MAY '70

It was the fall of 1967, in the midst of high anxiety and protest against the United States involvement in Vietnam. I was in my third year of college at Cal-State, Northridge, and working at Sears. Young, strong-willed, full of ambition and partying whenever the opportunity presented itself, my studies were soon affected. I was placed on scholastic and social probation. Already on edge and walking a fine line, I encountered one class that changed the direction of my life. A heated argument exchanged between classmates and me over the negative effects of America entering the Vietnam War. My classmates extolled the Far East and it's good side, this infuriated me, and I became appalled at the demeaning of the United States. Defiantly I stood up in defense and announced, " I'll go, see for myself and come back and tell you." Realizing my anger and actions may have consequences I turned and walked out. I did exactly as I promised, driving to the nearest recruiting office, where I enlisted in the U.S. Army.

I never questioned signing up that day in the military service. Our grandmother, who raised us, was very patriotic. Because our dad was deaf and unable to serve in the military, she taught us to honor our country and sing the Star Spangle Banner. Patriotism was instilled in us as children of the fifties, so I was confident in doing the right thing. I soon was off to boot camp at Ft. Ord, California for six weeks of intense training both physically and mentally. I describe boot camp as 'a life-changing event, designed to instill discipline.' My three years of college, allowed me to have the temporary rank of Corporal, and I was a squad leader during basic training. This position had more to do with my age of 22, compared to the majority of 17-18-year-old recruits.

After a few months at Fort Ord, I asked to go to Viet Nam. It was October of 1968 when I flew on a World Airways MAC flight from Oakland California to Vietnam. When asked how I felt while flying to the warzones in Vietnam, I honestly had "raw fear, masked by bravado." After we landed in Tan Son Nhut, we were directed immediately off the plane and onto a bus. It was hot and humid and at our first stop was a vendor selling beer or ice cream. A cold beer sounded pretty good and went down easily. However, to this day, I can relate a chronic intestinal problem to that first drink in Vietnam. Arriving at the barracks, I settled in with my work assignment at the 32nd Medical Depot as an Administrative clerk. Focused and diligent in all my duties; I also accepted a position to manage the base bar for the EM-NCO's (enlisted men's club) Successfully balancing the budget and keeping the inventory stock made for "happy soldiers." Profits allowed me to purchase entertainment and sound equipment as well as provide great steaks. I soon was selling two beers for five cents. A businessman was born!

The 176 Veteran Detachment Barracks had trained dogs to defend and protect; the dogs were also able to detect poison food, especially the meats that were brought into camp. Somehow, I was able to commandeer the top steaks that were good but "mistakenly mismarked questionable." We happily served and ate those delicious steaks for the EM-NCO parties and functions. All things were possible in a warzone, and you learn to be inventive and adaptable. There was a whirlpool of activity each day, as we bartered for everything, including rides and other provisions.

Most of my 13-month tour was with the 32nd Medical Depot in Cam Rahn Bay, which was located in a well-sheltered harbor. This harbor was of great strategic importance to our efforts in the war. I had TDY (temporary duty assignments) and spent some time at other bases. I was sent to Qui Nhon, then Nha Trang, both of these places were main military ports. The other bases were Dong Tam, Bien Hoa, Long Bien, and Pleiku. My last five months were spent with the 67th Evac Hospital in Qui Nhon.

After being in Vietnam for six months, our older sister informed me, that Betty was flying the MAC flights in and out of Vietnam. My first reaction and thoughts were her safety. I was concerned about where she was flying in Vietnam. I knew that the airstrips in Cam Rahn Bay were safely controlled and the base was secure for all commercial aircraft to land. Both U.S. and South Korean military patrolled the perimeters.

I can't remember how we made contact prior to her flying into Cam Rahn Bay, but the days Betty flew into the base, ground personnel from the airport called to alert me that her flight was on descent and landing shortly. Without hesitation, I left my unit for the airport thinking, 'what were the odds of seeing a family member in Vietnam?' It had been years since we saw one another. Intently watching the Continental aircraft approaching and knowing that my sister was onboard was a thrilling moment. Seeing each American commercial plane was a nostalgic link to home. This was particularly true because we didn't see many round-eyed women.

I eagerly waited on the tarmac until all the soldiers deplaned; there she was in her polished pink uniform dress, wearing hat and gloves. Her red patent shoes gave her the yellow brick road look. We hugged and smiled as she held on to her hat being caught by hot winds. We

BEHIND MY WINGS

shared as much as possible in the brief ten minutes,
feeling the love of a brother and sister. She then turned
and ran back up the stairs, not looking back, hiding her
tears. The commercial aircraft were never on the ground
for more than thirty minutes. The war had not slowed
down, and neither did the MAC flights. I wasn't aware of
how many came and left, but it was a daily flow of soldier's
replacements. All the military branches operated in and
out of our base.

Fortunately, this was not the last time Betty and I were
able to see one another. There were at least three more
opportunities when we exchanged hugs and smiles.

My purpose to be in Vietnam was clear to me at the
time. I received DEROS orders (Date of Estimated Return
from Over Seas) for assignment to Fort Rucker, Alabama.
Knowing my liberal bias, I thought this stateside assignment
could present challenges, so I elected to extend my tour
for an additional six months. The benefit of this was the
opportunity to choose my in-country duty station and also
shorten my commitment to the Army by five months. An
early out seemed very attractive at the time.

My R&R took me to Bangkok, Taipei and Hong Kong.
I also had a 30-day leave at home between deployments
from the 32nd Medical Depot to the 67th Evac Hospital.
Between duty assignments, I was able to come back to the
States to be with our older sister and family before she
delivered her second child. This 30-day leave allowed me
to be home for both Thanksgiving and Christmas in 1969.
Unfortunately, I returned to Vietnam before the birth of
our niece, Vikki. All in all, my duties were necessary and
sometimes quite demanding. Yes, I encountered and saw
unforgettable things, but those memories I have put aside.

Returning to the states after serving two tours of duty
in Vietnam, I finished college earning degrees in political

science and urban planning. As I recall my transition back home, was slow but progressive.

Bob received various commendations including the Bronze Star for his military service. We were thankful he came back alive. He continually gives to organizations in his community; he is proud of his service and proud still of his country. A success at his job, Bob remains thankful for the many blessings in his life, mostly his family, children, and grandchildren. He continues to be reminded how God spared his life.

Thank you for being a special brother not only to me but to our sister, Shirley. Sibling love is unconditional, your family and friends are very proud of your service. —Betty

"Trust in the Lord with all your heart
and lean not on your own understanding"
Proverbs 3:5

Chapter 14

COUSINS IN COMBAT

For every story told, there are thousand more untold. Giving honor and acknowledgment to our military men and women is the right thing to do! I had many cousins and uncles over the course of generations who served in the Armed Forces. Some have been able to share their stories and others did not want to remember. From the beginning, our families have served in the Armed Services. I am thankful and grateful to each family member who has served and to those who are presently serving. The Granillo family was very large on my mother's side, linked to the Ruiz families. The following stories are from family members, told by them.

Larry Larios, my cousin by marriage, shared his story of Vietnam while at a family reunion ... I joined the Navy while in high school. However, prior to signing up, I had been involved with a gang and was doing wrong things. My path and destination could have been short lived. While still in high school, I excelled in machinery and math. One of my teachers took notice of me and encouraged me to join the wrestling team. My teacher was a Navy Reservist and began to groom me. He saw my abilities and he said the Navy is looking for young men with courage like me. The list of enlisted men was very long at the time. Thinking I was safe, I signed up in my 11th year. A month after graduating from high school, I was called into the Navy.

An incredible story evolves, as my teacher and I were both assigned on the *USS Benetton*, which was stationed near Da Nang. I was placed in the position to work for the Central Intelligence Quarters as City Security Police for the Navy. I was the MP and when our ship would port, my duties found me on land roaming, keeping things secure.

In 1968, I vividly remember the riot that took place in downtown DaNang. It took all four branches of our Military Police to stop the riot. Personally, I believed the war in Hanoi could have been stopped in the first year but war and politics make money. Still to this day, I have flashbacks. Never take a soldier's service lightly, tread with kindness and honor.

Thank you, Larry! God did have his hand on you and you made our family proud with your military service.

Another of my cousins, Michael Granillo, has been a leader in our family for quite some time. With one uncle still remaining after 16 siblings have passed away, we all pay homage and respect to this cousin. He has taken the lead and has helped many of his own siblings.

He was in the Army and served in Vietnam from 1965 to 1966. He shared that on his first flight into Vietnam a staff sergeant seated near him started crying when they were preparing to land. He knew right then what he was about to face was going to be very bad.

When I asked Michael some questions, he really was uncomfortable to speak about things that happened. He said, war is war and you have to separate your present life with things that happened in war. One thing, he did share was a battle that took place on a hill with his unit. He recalled ... We were being fired upon. My buddy who was in front of me was shot and fell back on me. I realized he was dead and just at that moment my whole world changed. We fought to survive, and counted the days to come home.

Michael received many medals, none of which he speaks about. He was wounded several times even was hit by shrapnel from a grenade. When he returned home, he never discussed his experience in Vietnam. His cousins and Michael's wife, Debbie, said it was private, so with that, we leave things alone.

Michael's family and friends played a very important role in his recovery and he was able to settle into the real world. With our older generation passing, he felt his place was to look out for his family members.

He and his wife do their best to continue to have family reunions and keep the family together. Did the war change him? Yes, it did! He came back with many sorrows and things that are difficult to talk about. However, he was able to go back into the work force and is thankful he had a wonderful career.

Michael continues to have a sense of humor and keeps our large family strong, filled with much laughter and love. Every Monday he sends all of us cousins a joke for the week.

Thank you, Michael, for your service, and love for your family. You are the light on the hill, representing God's love for his children. Bless you, love you! —Your cousin, Betty Jo

"A thousand may fall at your side, ten thousand at your right hand, but it will not come near you."
Psalms 91:7

Chapter 15

A PAGEANT QUEEN & HER BROTHER

USO TOUR TO VIETNAM AUGUST 1967
SHARON SINGSTOCK
MISS WISCONSIN 1965

In her own words ...

It took twelve years before I could really begin remembering back to that August of 1967. I had just walked out of the theatre near UCLA in Westwood, California having watched the movie, Apocalypse Now. The year was 1979 and suddenly my senses were back in the hot humid cloying fields of Vietnam. Flashbacks of my USO tour surged as I remembered the strange beauty of the jungles and the serenity of the South China Sea. I saw men my age lying in field hospitals, heard the din of helicopters and the sounds of troops fighting in the near distance. These were memories that had not surfaced until that day. All at once my eyes filled with tears recalling the return flight back to stateside. I was so appreciative of our freedom in this great country of ours that I wanted to kiss the ground when we landed.

Events in life can alter one's path, as did mine. Winning Miss Wisconsin in 1965 led me to a year of adventure, travel, and experiences that changed the course of my life. It was winter and I was a junior at the University of Wisconsin in Madison when I received a call from the Miss America Pageant in Atlantic City. It was an invitation to join the very first Miss America Pepsi sponsored USO tour to Vietnam. I could not believe my ears, there would be five of us to accompany the reigning Miss America 1967, Jayne Jayroe. It was an exciting opportunity taking place the following year and would not interrupt my education. I accepted and the preparations began over the next several months, beginning with the 21 vaccinations needed for traveling to Southeast Asia. We met up in New York City for wardrobe, photo shoots, rehearsals, and our farewell dinner with Joan Crawford. She was the head of Pepsi and they were the sponsors of the Miss America USO Pepsi tour. All of this was extraordinary from winning Miss Wisconsin to being asked to participate in the first Miss America USO tour to Vietnam.

Flying from New York to California, we boarded a MAC flight for the long twenty-one-hour flight to Vietnam. We had no idea what we were going to encounter, we spent countless hours on the flight practicing the songs and program in our minds. We landed at the airport of Saigon. As we exited the airplane, the heat hits you first, like a hot furnace then the steaming humidity. It was like a thick heavy, wet, hot blanket. It was August and Southeast Asia was just like the Okefenokee Swamp in our summers in the US.

Our first night was at the USO headquarters in Saigon, the official stopover for all the entertainers. It was there we met Army Captain Frank Lennon, who was to be our chief security officer and escort while in Vietnam. Honored for the assignment, Captain Lennon did a remarkable job keeping us out of harm's way and making sure we stayed on schedule. He succeeded except for one incident where a helicopter pilot who outranked him, commandeered us to perform for his men. A small heated argument arose between Captain Lennon and the pilot. The pilot prevailed and with a short diversion, we were flown behind the DMZ. It was raining when we landed and we traveled the rest of the way in jeeps. The downpour caused poor visibility and the driver told us he was very concerned about our safety in this area. Yes, we were fearful, but it was times like this when the men showed their bravado that we truly felt their protection. Shortly after we set up for our show, intelligence reported that they were expecting a mortar attack and we were immediately evacuated. Our hearts sank. Disappointed in not being able to do our show for these soldiers we also realized we would not be coming back to the DMZ area. The purpose of the USO tour was to entertain and boost the morale of our troops. Our show made this possible with our songs and music. Our performances and smiles brought light to the darkness of war. We visited hospitals, both on base and in the field and dined with soldiers in mess halls. We enjoyed our one-on-one time in conversation whenever possible. Collected names, addresses, and phone numbers bringing back personal messages to their families. That was one of the most poignant memories we achieved. This was a time before Internet or Skype and letters took days, even weeks to reach the states.

"What's Happening Back Home" was the title of our show. It was a mixture of dancing and musical songs from Folk, Broadway, and Rock and Roll. The show was fun, clean, and several of the commanding officers remarked that ours was a truly clean-cut show emphasizing the all-American girl. At some bases, as many as 12,000 soldiers turned out. At one camp men were sitting and standing for two hours. Some had climbed trees, some strapped themselves to a branch to be sure they could see.

At the LZ English base in Bien Hoa, south of Da Nang, some 600 men stood in pouring rain waiting for the show to start. The electrical system went out and with no sound system, the show was canceled. We had the guys come up on stage, shook their hands and talked to hundreds of them. We did this as much as time and conditions allowed. Traveling in shapeless fatigues and boots on all types of vehicles, we entertained every branch of the military. Our group flew in a variety of helicopters with armed guards hanging out the sides, giving us an unparalleled bird's eye view of the country.

When we traveled to the aircraft carriers *USS Intrepid* and *USS Constellation,* we were met by fighter jets and escorted to the respective ship. Since it was the 24th Birthday of the Intrepid, our USO tour planned a surprise for the men, by having Miss America jump out of a birthday cake. This was a definite wow factor and the guys loved her. We performed in the ships giant airplane hangers with troops literally hanging from the overheads. We watched as fighter jets were catapulted off the runway to warzones and later were told some never returned. Our purpose and stamina grew from every incident we encountered. We pressed on, giving our best performance in every show.

A heart stopping moment was when we were catapulted off the ship Constellation in a plane. The thrill of ascent caused our stomachs to drop and our hearts to flutter. The spectacular view below of the South China Sea and the mountains of North Vietnam in the distance was breathtaking. The pilots flew us to Da Nang where we did an afternoon show at Freedom Hill and later that evening took a boat across the Da Nang River to have dinner at General Cushman's home. After our dinner, we headed down to the dock but were instructed to retreat as "Charlie" (Viet Cong) had been found in the water near the boat. For our safety, we were transported via the road to the villa where we were staying. There was only one bridge left, the military and Captain Lennon worried that "Charlie" used this incident as a decoy to force us back to the road where they may have planted mines. To protect us against a possible ambush, we were put in an ambulance transport with an armored car in front and one behind us. Fortunately, we arrived back at the Villa without an incident. By the way, this was no Villa, we had no water and the toilet was overflowing. Somehow we managed to sleep in spite of the conditions without a complaint. We knew there were soldiers who were sleeping in worse conditions out in the jungles.

Each day took us to new destinations with various stops when appropriate. We were particularly impressed with the reaction from the troops at Lai Khe. I did not plan to be so deeply touched by the courage and the character of our troops at this facility. This was the last point on the front for the men; they were either going out to the battlefields or had just returned. When the soldiers went out it was for four months, so you can see why they were most enthusiastic at our shows. They were alive and thankful. Emotions were high and even through a heavy downpour shrank our dresses, we never missed a beat. The guys "hooah" it all! We found their morale simply terrific. All of us agreed that we have never played to a more appreciative and wonderful audience. Everywhere we traveled the sense of community and comradery was like no other. Ironically war creates its own social environment among soldiers.

Midway through our tour, we went to a base camp that was carved out of the dense rugged jungle. It was the Black Horse Regiment of the 11th Armored Cavalry. I had the wonderful surprise of meeting their Chaplain Woodworth who I had met in Wisconsin on the occasion of my grandparents' 60th Anniversary. It was a divine appointment and we were able to have a special lunch together and afterward, he gave me a tour of the chapel.

The USO tour had been a remarkable trip but the most exciting moment was when arrangements were made for my brother David and me to meet. He was a Lieutenant Junior Grade on the Navy gunboat, *USS Gallup*—a powerful and compact gunboat based in Da Nang.

It had been a year since we had seen one another. He had been stationed in Seattle Washington when I was at the University of Wisconsin in Madison. The very first night we landed in Saigon, at 2400 hours I received a call from him. He sounded great and we talked for about thirty minutes. He told me in October he would be deployed to the Destroyer Division, then back to the states, hopefully in time for the birth of his son. He shared that he had received the Vietnamese Gallantry Cross Medal for combat action during a battle he and his crew fought in Sa Ky. My heart burst with pride and love for him. I prayed that during the tour we would be able to see one another.

Logistics and concerns arose whether Dave's gunboat would be able to reach the base where we were performing. Finally, at the very end of our tour, the *Gallup* was rerouted to Cam Rahn Bay. I remember it was raining as we flew from Na Trang to Cam Rahn Bay when they told me that my brother was meeting our plane. My heart was thrilled, anticipating seeing him face to face. When the aircraft came to its final stop, I wanted to be the first one off when the main cabin door opened.

Stepping down the stairs, I could hardly wait to put my arms around him. He informed me that arrangements had been made for him to be my escort for the next two days. God's timing was perfect to have my brother as my special escort; I felt so very thankful and blessed. That same day we toured the Gallup, then returned to base for dinner before performing in front of 10,000 troops. We were exhausted yet exhilarated at the same time. After our performance, we were invited for cake at the General's quarters. I was enjoying every moment with my brother by my side, what a glorious night.

The next morning we left at 0830 to have breakfast with the crew on the gunboat with a special church service on board by Chaplain Woodworth. God had answered my prayers for my brother and me to be together and incredibly standing with the Chaplain whom we both knew. It was an emotional time for us and for the guys. Before my brother and I parted, we were able to make a MARS (Military Auxiliary Radio System) telephone call to our mother at her office back in Oshkosh. What a thrill for her to hear our voices and to know that we were together and safe in Vietnam. I was thankful that my brother and I were able to see one another and prayed he would return home safely. It was with difficulty we said our goodbyes and I was off to perform our last show at the 6th Field Convalescent Hospital. As our tour ended, we boarded a plane back to Saigon. We gave special thanks to Army Captain Frank Lennon, who was then assigned to Special Forces.

The return flight home to the US was long and exhausting. We had performed 18 shows in nine and half days, traveling from base to base. What a whirlwind! The performances throughout Vietnam are imprinted memories that forever will remain in my heart and mind. We were eyewitnesses to our soldiers who served, fought and protected, no matter what the conditions or sacrifices.

Normalcy soon returned and our family rejoiced when my brother Dave returned home safely from Vietnam. Thanks and gratitude to the Miss America Pageant, the USO Organization, and Pepsi Cola. It was an honor and privilege to help boost the morale of our brave troops in Vietnam. Thank you for serving, "Welcome Home." OOH-RAH! —Sharon Singstock Bury

"A wife of noble character who can find?
She is worth far more than rubies. Her husband has full
confidence in her and lacks nothing of value."
Proverbs 31: 10-11

DAVID SINGSTOCK
LIEUTENANT (JG) US NAVY
VIETNAM 1967

Authors Comment: Our Vietnam Heroes came from all across America. David Singstock was raised in the Midwest state of Wisconsin, America's Dairyland. He was an all-American, clean-cut young man whose military aspirations began at seventeen. As a young boy, Dave's sights had been on the Navy, his story begins.

CHILDHOOD ASPIRATION BY DAVID SINGSTOCK

I was a young ambitious teenage entrepreneur, cutting grass, shoveling snow, and delivering newspapers. I saved enough money to buy my mother a Sears's sewing machine. When I was eight years old, I joined the Cub Scouts and then the Boy Scouts. I am proud to say, at 13 I became the youngest in the country to receive the Designated Eagle Scout Honor.

Sailing, ships, and the sea had always been my dream as a young boy growing up in Wisconsin in a city surrounded by lakes. My room was a typical boys room filled with military posters and ships of both WWI and WWII. My parents encouraged me to set my standards high and pursue my military aspirations. I was so thankful they taught me discipline, humility, and faith in God. Throughout my teenage years, I worked and studied hard preparing myself hopefully for one of the Military Academies. At seventeen, I enlisted in the Naval Reserve with the support and help of my family. Graduation ceremony at my high school was a highlight for me as I had received appointment letters to both the Naval and Merchant Marine Academy's. I made the decision to accept enrollment at the Merchant Marine Academy.

Discipline as a military officer, classes, sailing, and long nights of studies consumed me for three years. After two months at sea with the Military Sealift Command, I returned then to the Maine Maritime Academy, where I earned a degree in Marine Engineering and finished academically with a high score. I was thrilled to graduate second in my class, an honor I did not take lightly. Attending a Service Academy and serving in the Navy as an Officer was a fulfillment of my lifelong desires and dreams. As a young man, my compass was set. I sailed on the seas, unaware years later I would rendezvous with my sister in a small village called Cam Rahn Bay, Vietnam.

The Vietnam War had begun and I did have thoughts of being deployed. Then in 1964 I was called to active duty and assigned to the USS *Mattabasset* (AOG-52) known by some as the "fueling lady," a Navy tanker providing petroleum products to Naval Forces. I spent a year and a half on board this incredible ship, applying my skills as a licensed Marine Engineer and Officer of the Deck Formation Steaming, (OODF). The *Mattabassett* was equipped to logistically supply lube oil, fuel, and special aviation fuel for deployed ships and helicopters of the 6th Fleet. I was the ship's Chief Engineer responsible for liquid cargo operations, main propulsion, firefighting, and damage control. During that period of time, we refueled numerous ships, as well as visited ports in Spain, Italy, Greece, and France.

After we returned to Little Creek, VA, we were deployed over to the Arctic Circle. During that deployment, we all became "Blue Noses" (a term given to all who have crossed the Arctic Circle). Our missions in that area were fueling and supporting other logistic functions for a division of Destroyer Escorts (smaller warships). Once back in homeport the *Mattabasset* was assigned to the Norfolk Naval Shipyard for a regular overhaul. During that time, I was promoted to LT Junior Grade (JG) and subsequently assigned as Executive/Engineer Officer to the USS *Plainview* (AGEH-1), an ocean-going experimental hydrofoil. It was under construction in Seattle, Washington and because of an ongoing west coast electricians' strike, all work stopped on the *Plainview*. Due to the strike, the Bureau of Naval Personnel informed me that I would shortly receive orders to Vietnam as the Weapons/Engineer Officer on the newly constructed Gunboat *Gallup* (PG-85).

When these orders came for Vietnam, I had been preparing myself emotionally and mentally. My new orders took me to San Diego, California where I went through pre-Nam training on a high-powered gunboat. This gunboat was designed for high speed patrolling in shallow waterways, able to maneuver and operate with incredible speed. This new assignment as the Weapons/Engineer Officer was now for unchartered waters in an unknown warzone. I can honestly say that deployment to Vietnam struck a chord of the reality of combat. It was the anxiety of the unexpected or fear of the unknown that plagued all of us as we faced combat duty.

Studying the unfamiliar terrain of Vietnam and its varied coastal waters was a new challenge. My mind wondered ahead of what I might encounter. Setting sail was going to be a challenge. The sea is unforgiving and unpredictable. Gunboats were not equipped to travel the expanse of the ocean alone. Leaving San Diego's Naval base, we traveled with the *USS Catamount*, a landing ship dock as a fuel support/guide ship. The plan was to leapfrog across the Pacific Ocean and South China Sea. The *Gallup* and *Ashville*, two gunboats would run on gas turbine propulsion during the day and then go on diesel propulsion at night waiting for the *Catamount* to catch-up. We would then refuel the next morning and back to leapfrogging. The weather was never good. We traveled in rough seas most of the journey. The *Gallup* pitched and rolled making it difficult to function. Weather permitting, we fired all ordnance (gunnery drills) in preparation for future combat operations. When we left San Diego, we gave ourselves a motto, "HAVE GUNS WILL TRAVEL." It took courage and physical strength handling the gunboat. We would allow the *Catamount* sailors to board and sail with us on the *Gallup*. The gunboat ride was tough and very demanding on your equilibrium. Unaccustomed to feeling the waves, many of the sailors became seasick. Our assigned ports were Hawaii, Guam, and the Philippines before sailing to Cam Rahn Bay, Vietnam. We were the first "Jet Powered" high-speed gunboats and each port was filled with soldiers and sailors looking at our new gunboat. When we arrived in Guam, the *Ashville* suffered a major engineering casualty and had to remain in port for repairs, while the *Gallup* and *Catamount* proceeded to the Philippines and then onto Vietnam. It was a rough trip over to the unexpected warzones. Shortly after our arrival, the *Gallup* was reassigned to the homeport of DaNang where we were put on coastal patrol.

Our job was to stop North Vietnamese vessels from resupplying their forces by sea. We boarded all coastal crafts looking for contraband, weapons, and ammunition and also were sent to rescue downed pilots who ditched or were shot down near our patrol sector. Being a jet-powered gunboat, we could get to a search area very quickly. Every mission placed us in danger, but our adrenaline was always high with expectations to find one of our pilots. We would find parts of the aircraft, in a few cases helmets and other debris. Unfortunately, we never recovered a downed pilot.

Fear of the unexpected kept us always on edge. Rest was hard to come by. The hot and sticky humid days were filled with continual encounters and the nights were long and dangerous.

It was July 1967 where we tracked, intercepted, and captured a North Vietnamese gun running trawler. The day began when we departed DaNang in search of the trawler reportedly leaving North Vietnam and heading south along the coast. A normal trawler was a fishing vessel, quite common to see on the waters. We sighted the trawler using an infrared telescope and followed her to the rendezvous point/destination at the mouth of the Sa Ky River. We were informed that the trawler was to meet up with about 1200 North Vietnamese Regulars and provide them with weapons and ammunition. When the trawler was near her rendezvous point we lit her up with flares and over a loud speaker commanded her to stop. When the trawler crossed our path, we could see activity on her deck and gunfire erupted. We returned fire and the battle began. Large guns were mounted on her main deck, which previously had been covered with fishing nets. During the combat engagement, my job was on the port/starboard small bridge wings maneuvering the gunboat to the most advantageous position for direct hits on the trawler.

At dawn's first light, the trawler had run onto a reef engulfed in flames and the crew dead. The trawler was refloated off the reef and then inspected for contraband. We found important documents, ammunition, and rifles, enough to equip a small North Vietnamese army. The trawler was towed to DaNang and put on display with the recovered cache. This was the battle of Sa Ky and she was the first trawler captured during the war. This endeavor was a joint naval mission with other coastal patrol crafts.

As I remember, a month later, my mom told me that my sister Sharon was asked to become part of a Miss American Pepsi USO tour to Vietnam. The previous year she had been Miss Wisconsin and runner-up to Miss America. I was in awe and excited with this news, but how and when could we rendezvous? Sharon was with a scheduled troupe and I was on coastal patrol on the *USS Gallup* gunboat from the DMZ south, inside I Corps. When the time came closer to the arrival date of the Miss America USO tour, I began to look at their schedule and also where *Gallup* would be. When I found out that Sharon had landed in-country, I was ecstatic to be able to get a phone line to call her. It was wonderful to hear her voice since we had not talked for over a year. Somehow, when you least expect it, the powers that be will actually work in your favor. Yes, Sharon was going to be in Cam Rahn Bay and the Gallup was redirected to that port for R & R. I was thrilled to be able to greet my sister and meet the troop of beauties.

Arrangements were made for me to be at the US Air Force airfield in Cam Rahn Bay when the plane came in for landing. As the doors opened and the stairs attached to the airplane, tears filled my eyes seeing my sister deplane. We hugged and kept hugging as she introduced me to the other pageant winners and chaperone. Who would have ever thought growing up that you would be in a warzone with your sister? Feeling quite proud of her and meeting in this unbelievable place, I was given the assignment to be her personal escort during her stay. I brought her and the girls to the Gallup for a tour and to meet the crew. The gunboat crew and fellow "Swifties" (Swift Boat sailors) went wild because that area had not been blessed with a visit from such gorgeous women. That evening, I was most impressed with the troop's performance at the very over-crowded air base. I thought to myself, there was my young sister who looked so beautiful performing with the USO Miss America Pepsi tour. The soldiers were pumped. The atmosphere was filled with roaring applause and whistles for the girls from home. It was an awesome electrifying night! The next morning we had services on board the *Gallup* with the Chaplain from Green Grove Wisconsin. A photographer from the Navy Times, that I believe may have been following the tour, took a picture of Sharon and me by the *Gallup*. The picture was in a later issue of the paper. One of the highlights of Sharon's and my visit was when we called our mother at her job at the Oshkosh Northwestern Newspaper. It was great to hear our mom's voice and she too was thrilled to know that we did get together and were safe. Sharon's visit came to an end too quickly. Before I knew it, I was kissing her goodbye and she was off to entertain more of the troops. I sadly watched her plane depart and even though our visit was short, it was a moment in time, I will hold dear for the rest of my life. The USO tour gave us a long-awaited break, taking our minds momentarily off the war, rest that was needed, and entertainment that was so appreciated before returning to the Gallup and back to the realities of war. Days lead to months, conflicts and battles through the scorching sun and downpour of rain, my tour finally ended in Vietnam.

I continued my Naval career serving in many significant assignments both at sea and on shore. I served as the Project Officer for the first Guided Missile Frigate, *USS Oliver Hazzard Perry*, where I met John Wayne at the ship's launching. I was also put in charge of the restoration of the *USS Stark* after she was hit and severely damaged by two Iraqi Exocet Air-to-Surface Missiles during Operation "Ernest Will." During Desert Shield and Desert Storm (Iraqi War), near the end of my career, I served as the Senior Technical Advisor to the Royal Saudi Naval Forces under

General Schwarzkopf. As Director in Missile Defense, I also served as the United States Senior Naval member to the Joint Chiefs of Staff commissioned United States/ Saudi Arabian Joint Security Review Group. Physical assaults from the "Gulf Syndrome" continue to attack my health attributed to "Scud Missile" launched attacks, toxic chemicals, and breathing smoke fumes from the oil field fires in Kuwait.

I retired as a Commander in 1993, receiving many personal decorations, service and foreign awards. To this day, I proudly wear my Vietnam Veteran's hat as I WELCOME HOME other Vietnam Vets and acknowledging the many people who continue to stop and thank me for my service. It was an amazing career. My retirement days are filled with community and volunteering projects.

Thank you Commander David Singstock and the crew of the *USS Gallup* for your incredible service to the United States Navy. We thank you. From the families of all the downed pilots, thank you for your search and rescue missions. You served and gave all to your country; you are highly esteemed and admired by all who know you. Thank you, God's Blessings to you.

"Be on your guard; stand firm in the faith;
be men of courage; be strong."
1 Corinthians 16:13

Chapter 16

HEROES OF MANY WARS

LIEUTENANT GENERAL RICHARD CAREY
UNITED STATES MARINE CORPS
ENTERED MARINE CORPS: 1945
RETIRED: 1983

ANTHONY A. WOOD
COLONEL TONY WOOD, MARINE CORPS
30 YEARS

As I sat in the auditorium among prestigious military veterans commemorating the 50th Anniversary of Vietnam, cameras, and excitement surrounded the room. Photos were being taken as the three distinguished men politely and humbly sat on the stage. I was handed a program that had their photos and bio's listed. It was an honor and privilege to be a part of this special event. I was so impressed to see how much admiration was given to each of them. One by one as they stood and walked to the podium, a standing ovation was given to them. I quickly took out my pen and notebook putting my writing skills to work. Let me introduce them to you, Colonel Anthony Wood (USMC Ret.) Lieutenant General Richard E. Carey (USMC Ret.) and Colonel Sam Johnson (USAF Ret.), a member of US Representative for Texas 3rd congressional district, serving in Congress since 1991. Colonel Johnson was a POW in Vietnam (Chapter 7-Price of Peace).

I felt privileged to be sitting with so many men who also served in Vietnam. As I looked around the room, I couldn't help but wonder who may have been on one of my flights either in or out of Vietnam. My part was so insignificant compared to these men, but because I was a part of this war, I am motivated to search out and write their stories. Hearing stories of Vietnam Vets brings about healing and strength to those affected by this war.

Today, I was witnessing a belated and well-deserved recognition, I can't go back and change history, but I can write new chapters. The room was filled with the memories as those sitting in the audience identified with these leaders. Lt. Gen. Carey commanded the evacuation of Saigon, Col. Johnson was a POW, nearly seven years, spending 42 months in solitary confinement. Col. Anthony Wood 30-year career in the Marine Corps and highly decorated with service medals. These three men rose to the top ranks and became incredible leaders of hundreds of thousands of warriors.

RICHARD CAREY
LIEUTENANT GENERAL, UNITED STATES MARINE CORPS
MARINE CORPS 1945-RETIRED 1983

As Lieutenant, General Richard E. Carey took the stage wearing his uniform with pride came a smile that greeted the standing ovation crowd. Even though he had officially retired from the Marine Corps in 1983, he was dressed in full uniform with his distinguished military service medals. As the applause continued, it was evident that he was a hero to his peers. Some may have known him or may have been under his command, but I was impressed and ready to take my notes. He began sharing his involvement and operation in the evacuation of Saigon in 1975. (Oh my, he who was standing before us was the pivotal person who made it happen. I remember watching the news in 1975 as they showed the evacuation.) His bio summarized his military career. Enlisting in 1945 in the Navy V-5 program with Marine Corps option when you earned your wings. When the war ended in 1945, he took a discharge and entered the next phase of his career enlisting in the US Marines. This was a soldier who knew he was going to make the Armed services his career.

During one of our phone interviews, Lt. Gen Carey shared that his father was confined to a VA hospital and he remembers visiting him. However, at the age of nine, he lost his mother and lived with various relatives, aunts and a grandfather. He tried to enlist in the Paratroopers, but he did not have anyone to sign for him. Determination led him to enlist in the service, which began his life-long career.

He graduated from the Naval War College as a 2nd Lt. and rifle platoon commander in 1948. He participated in combat operations in Korea, including the Inchon Landing and Chosin Reservoir and was wounded in action in 1951. After medical evacuation to the US, he served for a year as company commander at the Marine Corps Recruit Depot at Paris Island, South Carolina. His next assignment was to report to Pensacola, Florida for flight training and designated a Naval Aviator in 1953.

General Carey held a variety of squadron pilot and staff assignments including separate tours as an intelligence, maintenance, material operations and logistics officer in both attack and fighter squadrons. He served as the Intelligent Officer in the Office of the Commander-in-Chief Atlantic and later as the G-3 Officer, Fleet Marine Force Pacific.

His aviation command experience began in 1958 with Headquarters and Maintenance Squadron 32 while a Major, stationed at MCAS Beaufort, South Carolina. In 1966, he became a Lieutenant Colonel at Cherry Point, where he assumed command of the Marine Fighter Attack Squadron 513.

Following his assignment to the Republic of Vietnam, he commanded Marine Air Base Squadron 13 and later Marine Fighter Attack Squadron 115 during combat operations, while operating from Chu Lai Air Base. In 1971, he commanded Marine Aircraft Group 24, with the 1st Marine Brigade in Hawaii.

As Brigadier General in 1974, he became Assistant Wing Commander, 1st Marine Aircraft Wing, MCAS Iwakuni, Japan. In 1975, he concurrently commanded the 9th Marine Amphibious Brigade where he directed the Marine Corps participation in the evacuation of Saigon.

Lt. Gen. Carey was presented the Defense Superior Service Medal awarded for service in a position of significant responsibility. He was given the Distinguished Service Medal for exceptionally meritorious service to the Government of the United States in a duty of great responsibility as Commanding General, Marine Corps Development and Education Command, Quantico, Virginia, 1980-1983.

In addition to the Silver Star Medal, Gen. Carey's personal awards and decorations include: Legion of Merit with gold star in lieu of a second award; Distinguished Flying Cross; Bronze Star Medal with Combat "V" and gold star in lieu of a second award, Air Medal with Numeral 15; Joint Service Commendation Medal; Purple Heart Medal, Presidential Unit Citation with two Bronze Stars; Navy Unit Commendation Medal with one Bronze Star; and Meritorious Unit Commendation.

I recorded and wrote all these events, changes and acclamation to present to you a well-distinguished Lt. General Carey who was equipped and qualified to handle the evacuation of Saigon. It was an enormous task to conduct this massive operation.

In 1963 when America got into the fight in Vietnam, Lt. Gen. Carey was assigned a special mission to select potential battle locations and potential map locations for new airfields in addition to existing airfields in South Vietnam. He was well qualified to handle the enormous tasks of evacuations when it came in 1975. It took higher authority before evacuation could commence and each hour was critical. He gives accolades to General Wilson, also known as Smiling Cobra. General Wilson helped ensure the success of this evacuation with the use of the helicopters. Their goal was to evacuate as many as possible without casualties.

They both agreed only the most skilled helicopter pilots could help during this event. Weather conditions prevented flying, but with time running out as the North Vietnamese army drew closer, these brave, incredible pilots kept flying. They took as many people as possible, and danger faced them on every flight.

The South Vietnamese frantically sought any way to flee the carnage; they even used rowboats to get to the ships. This evacuation was at every level and going on at every base. Panic struck those who tried numerous ways to escape the coming onslaught that would be upon them. They took nothing with them, just the clothes on their back, holding on to their most precious treasure, their children, and family members. When the end became apparent, and there was no more room, mothers, fathers started handing their babies to those on the ships in hopes that they would survive and have a future.

Lt. Gen. Carey goes on to say the evacuation of Saigon was successful with over 100,000 evacuees who were rescued and placed on some of the 55 Naval ships. On each ship, there were 50 Marines to inspect every Vietnamese for weapons who boarded. Lt. General Carey goes on to say, 35 Marines were assigned on the top deck to help with needs and even assist in delivering babies if necessary. The General shares how proud he was of his Marines who kept the evacuations going. This incredible evacuation took place all within twenty-four hours.

Lt. Gen. Carey himself helped with the helicopter evacuations making several trips from the Philippines to Vietnam. He makes a strong statement at this point of his speech to us; "The Alamo" as it was called was the key to commencing and succeeding in this endeavor.

The evacuation continued to be scrutinized; they had to move fast in Saigon where they had to filter out the communist who wore civilian clothes. Lt. Gen. Carey pauses briefly as he looked out at his audience. "I didn't sleep during the many days of planning and through the operation. I napped at my desk; this operation seemed like a nightmare even while we were going through it."

The morning of the 29th at 0338 everything fell apart. During this evacuation, the North Vietnamese began to throw rockets. The evacuation intensified putting more pressure to expedite this endeavor. Lt. Gen. Carey stopped and shook his head as he shared the loss of two Marines, Corporals McMahon, and Judge who were killed in the rocket strikes. You could tell by his mannerism and voice inflections that losing those two fallen Marines was a huge sadness. He goes on to say, "There were a lot of heroic acts performed by my Marines." These men knew the danger of this enormous evacuation, and I did not want to lose even one.

The Air Force used many C-5s, and the Marines had C-130s to help complete the mission of the evacuation. Convoys were planned, and it took all the branches to accomplish this enormous effort.

Episodes after episodes were taking place as we were struggling to get our US Ambassador to evacuate. He did not want to leave behind any of his staff. All the helicopters were sent out to evacuate the Embassy as well as the Tan Son Nhut airport. The Vietnamese were coming over the walls, and that went on until the next morning. The time frame for the evacuation was rapidly coming to an end. As the North Vietnamese were getting closer, the Admiral on the USS Blue Ridge shut down the operation. I tried to get in touch with him on the amphibious ship but with no response; I had to go on a helicopter that took me to his ship to plead my case to continue the evacuation.

While in the combat control center, I received a call from Washington asking how many authorized evacuations remained to be evacuated. We radioed the Embassy control and were told there were still 800 to be evacuated. Washington then asked how many helicopters would it take? I answered 20 and directed by Washington, to only do no more than 20 lifts.

During the air evacuations, small boats were attempting to evacuate to the ship, to make room, the South Vietnamese helicopters were pushed off into the sea to accommodate the evacuees. The remaining Marines were still holding the fort. The last pilot, Jerry Berry picked up the last Marines, and that was the completing the end of the evacuation.

Our brave Marines did all they could, far beyond what was called for; we evacuated over 100,000 grateful Vietnamese. What did we leave? Hopefully, we left courage and faith. Many lost their lives, but many survived, owning gratitude for what our military tried to do for them.

"There is no easy part about war, this is my story, and God has been good to me."

Lt. Gen. Carey lives in the Dallas area; his mission is to encourage and share his military history. He always makes a point to thank and recognize those who served in the Armed Forces. He concluded by saying, "Military men and women are a breed like no one else." I am thankful and proud to have served both in the Korean and Vietnam wars, God Bless America.

"For I am convinced that neither death, nor life, nor angels, nor principalities, nor things present, nor things to come, nor powers, nor height, nor depth, nor any other created thing, shall be able to separate us from the love of God, which is in Christ Jesus our Lord."
Romans 8:38-39

COLONEL ANTHONY A. WOOD
MARINE CORPS-30 YEARS

Colonel Tony Wood enjoyed a distinguished career of over thirty years in the Marine Corps and continues to make contributions to his country as an inspirational speaker. He is the only Colonel in the US armed forces to have been decorated twice with the nation's second-highest Meritorious award, the Distinguished Service Medal. In 1968 he served his first tour in Vietnam as a platoon commander and advisor to the Korean Marine Corps Blue Dragon Brigade. In 1974, he commanded a joint casualty recovery team seeking MIA bodies in Laos, Cambodia, and Vietnam. He is well known as a member of the Special Planning Group charged with developing the plan for the evacuation of Saigon. Col Wood's last Marine Corps billet was as the first Commanding Officer of the Marine Corps Warfighting Laboratory.

Following retirement from the Marine Corps, Col. Wood joined the CAD (Collaborative Agent Design) Research

Center at California Polytechnic State University, in 1998, as Vice President/COO and Partner, in CDM Technologies Inc. During his twelve-year tenure at CDM, he designed a series of decision support systems to improve the speed and accuracy of decision-making for the U.S. Joint Staff and other military services, as well as civilian firms. He is an inspirational speaker who conducts leadership workshops around the country. He continues to serve in a variety of capacities on boards and as a consultant for executive decision-making.

"My son, preserve sound judgment and discernment, do not let them out of your sight; they will be life for you ..."
Proverbs 3: 21-22

Chapter 17

BAD START, NEW ENDING

PAUL BROWN
US ARMY

In Paul's own word ...

I cried most of my life growing up. As a young child, I would bury my face in my pillow and cry myself to sleep. You see, I was raised in a family filled with pain. God was not a part of our family. Dad was a heavy drinker and womanizer. My mom drank to cover the pain, which only brought about more pain. They fought—I mean they fought! I can remember my dad throwing my mother through a glass door and the doctor coming to the house to stitch her up. Yes, doctors did make house calls when I was growing up. My mother during one of their fights picked up a Colt 22 revolver and fired six shots at dad, missing him with all six shots from about 15 feet away.

At the age of 16, I quit school. I was a bad student and really did not enjoy school. I was an introvert with a lot of fear and there was no way I could stand in front of the English class to give a report. My fears were so great, that I would skip that class or even skip school that day. So I quit. Imagine God's sense of humor as years later he called me to be a pastor and teacher. About a year after I quit school, I enlisted in the U.S. Army, May 20, 1968. I enlisted in the Army to start a new life and to escape from where I was and what I might have become. I had started to drink and was smoking two packs of Marlboros per day.

I ended up at Fort Dix, New Jersey for basic and advanced infantry training as well as Light Equipment Maintenance. A mechanic was an easy gig for me. Within this time of training at Fort Dix, I was reassigned to a new MP (Military Police) company. A new MP company had formed and they needed men so I became an MP for about two months. It was at this time my orders came down to go to Vietnam. Wahoo! I was headed to war. I had no idea of where in-country I was going at that time. Shortly after that, we were loaded in a Seaboard World airliner for our long flight and yes, it was very long. Upon take off, the right side overhead luggage rack came down on our heads. Believe it or not, we did not turn around but continued on to our destination with a group of us holding up the rack. We landed in Fairbanks, Alaska where we stayed in the airport for two days while they fixed the luggage rack and other maintenance issues. Next, we were headed to Guam. We landed there and had to stay at the airbase airport another two days while some other maintenance issues were repaired. Guess they thought we were all going to die anyways so might as well fly them there on a piece of outdated junk. I swear that aircraft was held together with bubble gum and duct tape. We finally landed in Cam Ranh Bay, Vietnam to a noisy greeting. Scared? You bet!! Nearly wet my fatigues and I was not alone. Here we were, young boys, in a warzone with the sounds of war all around us and without weapons in our hands. Once again, we had another two-day delay as they kept us on the tarmac at Cam Rahn Bay before loading us onto busses to head to our destination, Phu Tai, in the central highland. I am thinking we are headed down an old dirt road in a warzone and again, I still do not have a weapon, wondering if this hand to hand combat stuff really works.

I was assigned to a large motor pool that repaired all types of vehicles as well as artillery, including Howitzers. I thought this would be a safe place and for the most part, it was except there was a mountain outside of the compound where the VC would pepper us with mortar rounds and B40 rockets. They fired on us with small arms fire on a regular basis. Many of the Vietnamese who worked on our compound during the day would shoot at us during the night. I caught one of them on the compound measuring off steps from the perimeter to the generator. It did not go well for him. One night during one of these attacks, I ran behind the mess hall for cover and found myself kneeling behind a large propane tank. I said to myself, "Run Paul, Run!"

The base that I was assigned wanted me to manage the parts supply depot. A high school drop out, with no real educational ability or experience, I said sure, why not. It was a mess, the Army records were bad, to say the least. After about three or four months, a four Star General flew in and conducted an inspection from which I received a 100% grade. I was promoted to Spec 4. Six months later, another four Star General inspection and again I received a 100% and promoted to Sergeant E-5. I was told that this was the first time anyone had received a 100% rating and I had received two. For this, I received the Bronze Star for meritorious achievement. This was the first time in my whole life that I felt worthy and good about myself. If you ever saw the movie Green Berets and remember Peterson, that was me. He always traded things or found a way to get things that were not authorized but made life easier. I would go to the docks at Qui Non and trade vehicle parts for cases of steaks and even one time a case of lobster. I am sure there were officers who were not happy when their shipment did not arrive.

I became a bartender at our base, NCO (non-commissioned officers) Club. I learned real quick how to make and mix every kind of drink. While there one evening, we were hit with mortar, B-41/41 rockets and small arms fire. Upon leaving to go to my duty station, a rocket hit a storage container just a few feet from me, knocking me down and out. When I woke up, I was scared to check my body parts as I was sure a leg or arm was missing. Totally unharmed and probably for the first time, I acknowledged and thanked God. I ended up spending two tours in Phu Tai and traveled throughout the country. I checked on other motor pools inventory and production lists and assisted them in getting their items in order. I hated the Anke Pass as we always took fire there and Bon Son was the worst because every time I was there, we were hit with everything Charlie had.

After 15 months in country, I started getting different letters from my mother. She had written before, but she started telling me about Jesus and her changed life. I thought, "Oh no, the booze has finally taken her last brain cell." The letters kept coming and she wrote with great excitement about her new life. As each letter arrived, it began to open me up to the reality of God and who Jesus was, the son of God.

Eight more months passed and a very unfortunate event happened in my life. I was driving a deuce and a half truck through the streets of Phu Tai and we were taking small arms fire. Just on the outskirts of town, a South Vietnamese soldier ran across the road in front of me, so close that there was no possibility of stopping. He was hit and immediately killed with his family watching. I instructed my M60 machine gunner to be ready as an angry crowd was quickly forming. We held them at bay until the MPs arrived and escorted us away from the site. When I arrived back at the base, the commander met me and told me I would be flying home the next day with an honorable discharge. This was to get me out of country and the Army, so that the Vietnamese government and the family could not come after me.

I arrived home December 20, 1970, happy to see my family, but sad for the family in Vietnam. Even today, my heart aches for them and what they saw. My mom had changed and looked peaceful. She began to tell me about her relationship with Jesus and about the small church she was attending. It was a small church in our town of 200. She asked me to go with her and I did after being home for a couple of weeks. Where else could I show off the custom made suits from Vietnam? I listened to the pastor who was an ex-outlaw biker tell of Jesus and His transforming power. On the evening of January 18, 1971, I knelt down by my bed in my room on the third floor of our home. A room with no heat and so cold a glass of water would freeze on my nightstand. I prayed a simple prayer saying, "Jesus, if you can do the things that the pastor said you could do, then do them in me." Well the room did not spin and lighting did not flash. I simply went to bed and in the morning when I awoke, I immediately took the pack of Marlboros from my nightstand and tossed them into the fireplace. I did not even dress, but ran down the stairs in my underwear with the family looking at me. I was changed; my life was transformed.

God had done a complete work in my life! From that moment, I never experienced the PTSD that so many suffer. Just two weeks after I gave my life to Christ, I was preaching. I had no Bible knowledge, just a changed individual who had met Jesus. An introvert who was now an extrovert standing in front of a congregation of people and sharing His love and life.

Paul Brown, retired Pastor, continues to spread the good news of Jesus Christ. Thank you for the years of service to your country and sharing your testimony.

"Now unto him that is able to do exceeding abundantly above all that we ask or think, according to the power that works in us,"
Ephesians 3:20

Chapter 18

THE NIGHT EVERYTHING CHANGED

"Here I am! I stand at the door and knock.
If anyone hears my voice and opens the door,
I will come in and eat with him and he with me."
Revelation 3:20 NIV

Times were changing as the war lingered and by 1972 it was beginning to wind down. Vietnamization was the United States' policy, a transition, giving the South Vietnamese government responsibility to carry on, allowing the withdrawal of American troops. It took three years and even on the last day of the final evacuation in Saigon 1975, we lost two more Marine soldiers as they were helping many to escape.

For me, two years of flying the MAC Operation was long and challenging. Continental Airlines only wanted us to fly these flights for one year. They said it was due supposedly for our well being. Little did I realize how true this would be for me. After transferring back to domestic flights, it was a stark contrast for me. I felt enveloped, in a time warp—a dichotomy from being surrounded by soldiers in the warzones. This change seemed strange and out of sorts. I needed some transitional time as battle scars and images of war lingered in my mind. Haunted by the harrowing sights and sounds of the war only led me to more parties and superficial living. My drinking continued back in the States as I desperately tried to find peace and love, however, the drinking and dating did not fill the void and pain in my life.

One night at a party in Manhattan Beach where drugs were prevalent and the punch bowl was spiked, I decided enough was enough. Grabbing my purse, I ran down to the beach and not wanting to touch the water, I stayed pretty far back from the waves. I felt all alone, somehow my world seemed so out of touch, what was I running away from? Realizing my pain was not only from the war, but everything from my childhood seemed to surface. I am not very good at crying, I get this big lump in my throat and can't see clearly because of my tears. But at that moment, I broke down and finally let go of all that I had been keeping inside of me for all these years.

The sound of the waves muffled my cries. As I was weeping, I looked up at the night stars and said, "God, are you real? I don't like it down here and want to come home." I was shocked at what I said and in that moment, I realized that I was talking with God. I was seeking Him and if He was real, I wanted to know Him. As I looked out over the ocean in the pitched darkness, suddenly, I saw a white foamy appearance on the water and peacefulness overshadowed me. Pretty radical for a person who did not even believe nor ever had a relationship, let alone give God the time of day. I had not taken any drugs nor did I drink the Kool-Aid. All I know is that I spoke to God for the first time and something inside of me woke up. That night I was finally seeking God, clueless as to who He was, clueless that He created everything. How could I have known? I was living in my own world, totally oblivious to Him. I was seeking God that night on the beach and I found Him.

"Ask and it will be given to you;
seek and you will find; knock
and the door will be opened to you.
For everyone who asks receives;
he who seeks finds;
and to him who knocks, the door will be opened."
Matthew 7:7

As I looked down at my toes in the sand, I saw footprints that were facing mine. As I was staring at them, the ocean waters came up to where I was standing and washed them away without getting my feet wet. I turned around staring at the lights on the beach houses and I heard this still small voice say, "You'll never be alone again." I was stunned and felt a surreal peace. It was a close encounter of the most personal kind. God heard my cry and desperate plea. I walked slowly back to my car because I had no desire or need to go back to the party and drove home.

My life changed that night. I was perplexed, shaken up, but I heard from God. Life altering events took place after that night. Several days later, I went to visit some old friends and while driving home, I said to God, "Maybe all this was an illusion or something?" So, I repeated what I had said that night on the beach, "God, if you are really real show me yourself." When I arrived home, barely putting my purse down, there was a knock at my front door. I opened the door to find three people who asked if they could come in and talk to me about God. Stunned and surprised I let them in. All three of them sat tightly in my love seat while I sat on a footstool facing them. As they began to talk, tears ran down my face. I didn't say much, only tried to listen, thinking to myself, they were clueless as to why I was so emotional or were they? God had immediately answered my prayers. They returned for several weeks, same time, same day, not once asking me to go to church with them or leave me any brochures. They just told me all about God and his son Jesus who died on the cross for my sins. It was quite remarkable. Then on their last visit, they said they would not be coming back anymore. I seemed to accept that, however, I couldn't help but wonder if they had been messengers or angels, sent by God. I then started praying asking God where do you want me to go to church?

During this interval I had visited one church but cried so much, I had to leave. Because of my lifestyle, I felt unworthy and unclean. Then, one night I got down on my knees and like a dam that had broken, tears flooded my eyes. I remained in my home for three days, crying and sobbing telling God how sorry I was for my lifestyle. On the third day, his small still voice spoke once again to me and said, "Get up, shower and get dressed, it's over." A miraculous change had taken place, I felt washed and clean, all my sins were gone—lifted and taken away. I knew in my heart God had completely forgiven me. I began reading the Bible and understood His unconditional love for me.

"Love covers a multitude of sins." Peter 4:8

I had a multitude of sins. My journey with God began slowly and yet I felt his presence and strong love. I came to understand who Jesus was and why he had to die on the cross for all of mankind's sins.

"For I know the plans I have for you, declares the Lord,
plans to prosper you and not to harm you,
plans to give you hope and a future."
Jeremiah 29:11

Oh, how I love that scripture. God is a personal God; He is real. He is alive and speaks to me, especially through His Word, the Bible.

He spoke clearly to me that night on the beach. He had been waiting for me. He helped me fight the battles that overpowered me, especially at night when I would try to sleep. Because I did not know about spiritual battles. A pastor prayed over me that in my sleep, I would be able to say, in the name of Jesus, go. I was able to say this and that old spirit has not been back. God sent Jesus, His Son to heal the brokenhearted, to proclaim freedom for the captives and release from darkness to light. That was me. I was weighed down with my past. Without a shadow of doubt, I was a new person. The Love of God will not take me where the Grace of God cannot keep me.

After going through this change, my coworkers, especially those who graduated with me from class noticed a remarkable change in my personality. If you were sitting on the jump seat with me on takeoff or landing, my conversation would always be about Jesus. I usually asked if they were born again? The Holy Spirit gave me a new boldness, I was concerned about all my coworkers and wanted them to know about a God who loves them. Later I wrote a small booklet, *Heaven Bound*, sharing my story of when I asked Jesus into my heart. Believe me, if we were going to have an emergency on board any of my flights, I would have easily used the PA system and made sure you knew where you were going to spend eternity.

There are not only the physical enemies of war but also the spiritual enemies. Battles and bondages are all around us, whether it's fear, despair, grief, sickness, or sadness, God's word speaks to each one of these. I experienced my healing and so can you. Realize God has a timetable for our lives. Remember Ecclesiastes 3:1-8 and Psalm 139. You were perfectly formed. I have learned to exchange all my inner battles with God's promises. He is an awesome God. There is an enemy who is the destroyer—he destroys families, he is a liar, speaks lies to our minds, and his name is Satan. God says:

"Greater is he who is in us, than he who is in the world."
1 John 4:4

I am a female, petite, reserved, but don't mess with me, because the mighty power of the God lives within me. His word says:

"And no weapon formed against me shall prosper."
Isaiah 54:17

If you have never asked Jesus into your life, you can right now. Simply say:

"Jesus forgive me of my sins, I believe you died on the cross for my sins and rose on the third day. Thank you for forgiving me and I forgive those who have done wrong to me. Fill me with your loving Spirit, guide and direct me the rest of my life as I start my journey with you. Thank you, in Jesus name, Amen."

It was a glorious day when I said that prayer. You have been born again if you prayed it. If you have a Bible, start reading the book of John. Pray to God every day, He loves our prayers. Remember when I started praying about where God wanted me to go to church? At the same house, there came again a knock at my front door. When I opened it, a young man was standing there. He introduced himself as pastor and said he was starting a church a block away. He invited me to come as it was brand new. I did and through that small congregation, I was led to another home group where I began my walk with God. They were wonderful people who loved me unconditionally and helped me to know God. A funny thing about that pastor, the house had a back door and after he finished talking with me at the front door, there was a knock at my back door, I opened the back door to find him standing again, we both laughed and I was so thankful to him and his wife for taking me under their wings as a brand new Christian. I have forgotten their names, but God knows them well and has a special reward for them in Heaven.

Chapter 19

WINGS OF HEALING

God in His most loving and gentle manner began healing all my brokenness, layer after layer, from childhood to my young adult years. He filled me with His love and forgave me of all my sins. I felt His love and peace as I walked this new journey with Him. I began hearing teachings on forgiving those who have wronged, violated, or stolen from me. I struggled to forgive my stepfather—how could I just forgive him? But walking with God now required me to obey this commandment. God knew I needed time. I remember working a flight and I had a few minutes before I had to take my jump seat for landing. I sat in a First Class seat, looking out the window, and this thought overwhelmed me. Slowly, I whispered, "I forgive you _____." I must have repeated it 20 times. Each time I said it, I felt better and better. When I finished and took my jump seat, the weight of the heavy burden I had carried for so long had been completely lifted. In those few moments I had been set free by the power of God. My stepfather was still alive. Even if he hadn't been, just by saying, "I forgive you" was enough to release me.

Shortly after that experience, my stepfather saw a change in me and said, "I have my daughter back, thank you, Lord." Then he shared his encounter with the Lord where he asked for forgiveness and turned his life over to Him as well. He quit drinking and gave up smoking. God truly did a work in his life. There was no more hate or anger, a genuine forgiveness took place in me. My stepfather passed away and I know he is in Heaven, as a forgiven man, able to hear, walk, and speak.

God can heal our minds and bodies. Forgiveness is the key to unlocking the doors of pain, loss, and trauma. Step by step, I continue to receive healing from all my past relationships. Above all, God says in his Word:

"For if you forgive men when they sin against you, your heavenly Father will also forgive your sins."
Matthew 6:14

It's probably difficult to understand a God who loves us so much that He sent His Son to die on the cross for us. His death takes away our sins from the past, present, and future. He gives us a rich meaningful life and freely gives us His Holy Spirit to guide and direct us in all our ways. I experienced healing, hope, and restoration and so can you, through Jesus Christ who heals every infirmity.

Chapter 20

HEAVEN BOUND, SAFE LANDING

My story is God's Glory. I share my story to remind others that God loves each one of us, wherever we are and whatever we have done. I know that I am heaven bound, not based on my works or how good I am, but simply believing and receiving Jesus as my Lord and Savior.

Jesus makes it pretty clear in John 14:6, where He says:

"I am the way and the truth and the life.
No one comes to the Father, except through me."

He taught me that He remembers my sins no more and has shown me how to walk in forgiveness. Life will still have disappointments and there will always be trials, but He told me that night on the beach I would never be alone.

We're never too old and it's never too late, only His love can change us. We may have thought that we've been this way all of our lives. We think that everything surrounding the war and our life circumstances have made us this way. God says it is never too late to begin your walk with Him. He desires a relationship with us, one that will take us further into a deeper walk with Him. Things of this world will get worse, but living in God's kingdom will preserve and fill our hearts with His unfailing love.

God gives us His peace the moment we ask him into our lives, peace that the world does not understand. God is and always has been the pilot of all my flights and of my life. He guides and directs me in an intimate loving way and allows me to commune with Him in a personal relationship. God loves us even in our sinful lives. His love is perfect, and He covers us in His grace, love, and mercy. Only God can heal

us and give us victory in those areas where we are weak and in bondage.
"I tell you the truth, no-one can see the kingdom of God unless he is born again. I tell you the truth, whoever hears my word and believes him who sent me has eternal life."
John 5:24

We're coming in for a landing. God does have a plan for each of us. He is our only hope. I pray as we continue on our journey that we all are heaven bound. See you there or meet you in the air! Godspeed to all who read this book.

"Whether you turn to the right or to the left,
your ears will hear a voice behind you saying,
"This is the way; walk in it"
Isaiah 30:21

To all the "Men of Valor" I give my love and respect. I pray for healing in your body and peace in your heart. You are my heroes, BJ, your flying buddy, WELCOME HOME!

A VIETNAM IMMIGRANT

On Saturday, July 24, 2010, the town of Prescott Valley, Arizona, hosted a Freedom Rally. Quang Nguyen was asked to speak on his experience of coming to America and what it means. He spoke the following in dedication to all Vietnam Veterans.

"Thirty-five years ago, if you were to tell me that I am [sic] going to stand up here speaking to a couple thousand patriots in English, I's [sic] laugh at you. Every morning, I wake up thanking God for putting me and my family in the greatest country on earth. I just want you all to know that the American dream does exist and I am living the American dream. I was asked to speak to you about my experience as a first generation Vietnamese-American, but I's [sic] rather speak to you as an American. If you hadn't noticed, I am not white and I feel pretty comfortable with my people. I am a proud US citizen and here is my proof (Holding up his naturalization papers). It took me eight years to get it, waiting in endless lines, but I got it and I am very proud of it.

I still remember the images of the Tet Offensive in 1968, I was six years old. Now you might want to question how a 6-year-old boy could remember anything. Trust me, those images can never be erased. I can't even imagine what it was like for young American soldiers, 10,000 miles away from home, fighting on my behalf.

Thirty-five years ago, I left South Vietnam for political asylum. The war had ended. At the age of thirteen, I left with the understanding that I may or may not ever get to see my siblings or parents again. I was one of the first lucky 100,000 Vietnamese allowed to come to the US. Somehow, my family and I were reunited five months later, amazingly in California. It was a miracle from God.

If you haven't heard lately that this is the greatest country on earth, I am telling you that right now. It was the freedom and the opportunities presented to me that put me here with all of you tonight. I also remember the barriers that I had to overcome every step of the way. My high school counselor told me that I cannot [sic] make it to college due to my poor communication skills. I proved him wrong. I finished college. You see, all you have to do is to give this little boy an opportunity and encourage him to take and run with it. Well, I took the opportunity and here I am.

This person standing tonight in front of you could not exist under a socialist/communist environment. By the way, if you think socialism is the way to go, I am sure many people here will chip in to get you a one-way ticket out of here. And if you didn't know, the only difference between socialism and communism is an AK-47 aimed at your head. That was my experience.

In 1982, I stood with a thousand new immigrants, reciting the Pledge of Alliance and listening to the National Anthem for the first time as an American. To this day, I can't remember anything sweeter and more patriotic than that moment in my life.

Fast forwarding, somehow I finished high school, finished college, and like any other goofball 21-year-old kid, I was having a great time with my life. I had a nice job and a nice apartment in Southern California. In some way and somehow, I had forgotten how I got here and why I was here.

One day I was at a gas station. I saw a veteran pumping gas on the other side of the island. I don't know what made me do it, but I walked over and asked if he had served in Vietnam. He smiled and said yes. I shook and held his hand. The grown man began to well up. I walked away as fast as I could and at that very moment, I was emotionally rocked. This was a profound moment in my life. I knew something had to change in my life. It was time for me to learn how to be a good citizen. It was time for me to give back.

You see, America is not just a place on the map, it isn't just a physical location. It is an ideal, a concept. And if you are an American, you must understand the concept, you must accept this concept and most importantly, you have to fight and defend this concept. This is about Freedom and not free stuff. And that is why I am standing up here.

Brothers and sisters, to be a real American, the very least you must do is to learn English and understand it well. In my humble opinion, you cannot be a faithful patriotic citizen if you can't speak the language of the country you live in. Take this document of 46 pages—last I looked on the Internet, there wasn't a Vietnamese translation of the US Constitution. It took me a long time to get to the point of being able to converse and until this day, I still struggle to come up with the right words. It's not easy, but if it's too easy, it's not worth doing.

Before I knew this 46-page document, I learned of the 500,000 Americans who fought for this little boy. I learned of the 58,000 names scribed on the black wall at the Vietnam Memorial. You are my heroes. You are my founders.

At this time, I would like to ask all the Vietnam Veterans to please stand. I thank you for my life. I thank you for your sacrifices and I thank you for giving me the freedom and liberty I have today. I now ask all Veterans, firefighters, and police officers to please stand. On behalf of all first generation immigrants, I thank you for your services and may God Bless you all. God Bless America—One Flag, One Language, One Nation Under God. For those who understand, no explanation is needed. For those who do not understand, no explanation is possible."

Quang Nguyen
Creative Director/Founder
Caddis Advertising, LLC

ABOUT THE AUTHOR

BJ Elliott Prior retired after 40 years as a flight attendant with Continental Airlines. She flew MAC Operations, transporting soldiers during the Vietnam War. Fighting through struggles in her growing up years, she finds the faith to carry her forward. Moving with compassion, she shares her life and the stories of "men of valor" during the Vietnam War. BJ says, "Flying as we knew it, changed drastically September 11, 2001. I was on a carefree London layover when I heard the horrific news about two airplanes hitting our Twin Towers! Stunned and shocked, our whole crew stayed together glued to the local BBC, and after five difficult days, we were allowed to fly back home. It was only after President George W. Bush urged all Americans to return to work on the following Monday that I was able to get back on an airplane. His words gave me courage and strength." She has never forgotten his words and prays that her book will bring the same courage and strength for healing and understanding to generations now and then. BJ and her husband are actively involved with their church as leaders and prayer warriors. They reside in Dallas/Fort Worth, blessed with an abundance of family and friends.

Linda Lou Coombs Wiese grew up in Oshkosh, Wisconsin and has had a wonderful career in the medical field. Her desire to become a writer was fulfilled as she collaborated with BJ to write Behind My Wings.

To obtain additional copies of the book go to:

WWW.BEHINDMYWINGS.COM

BJ is available to speak to Veterans, Churches, and Schools. For prayers or to leave comments, contact her at:

BJPRIOR@YMAIL.COM
817-723-6441

Made in the USA
Monee, IL
27 May 2022

97150108R00125